An Introduction to the Philosophy of Leisure

AN INTRODUCTION TO THE PHILOSOPHY OF *Leisure*

JASON HOLT

broadview press

BROADVIEW PRESS
Peterborough, Ontario, Canada

Founded in 1985, Broadview Press is a fully independent academic publishing house owned by approximately twenty-five shareholders—almost all of whom are either Broadview employees or Broadview authors. Broadview is supported by a collaboration with Trent University, a liberal arts university located in Peterborough, Ontario—the city where Broadview was founded and continues to operate. Broadview is committed to environmentally responsible publishing and fair business practices.

Library and Archives Canada Cataloguing in Publication

Title: An introduction to the philosophy of leisure / Jason Holt.
Other titles: Philosophy of leisure
Names: Holt, Jason, 1971- author
Description: Includes bibliographical references and index.
Identifiers: Canadiana (print) 20250180472 | Canadiana (ebook) 20250180480 | ISBN 9781554816743 (softcover) | ISBN 9781460408766 (ePUB) | ISBN 9781770489523 (ePDF)
Subjects: LCSH: Leisure—Philosophy.
Classification: LCC GV14 .H65 2025 | DDC 306.4/81201—dc23

Broadview Press handles its own distribution in Canada and the United States:
PO Box 1243, Peterborough, Ontario K9J 7H5, Canada
555 Riverwalk Parkway, Tonawanda, NY 14150, USA
Tel: (705) 482-5915
email: customerservice@broadviewpress.com

Broadview Press books are imported and distributed in the United Kingdom and European Union by:
Gazelle Book Services Ltd.
White Cross Mills, Hightown, Lancaster, Lancashire, LA1 4XS
sales@gazellebookservices.co.uk

European Union – Responsible Person (for official use only):
eucomply OÜ
Pärnu mnt 139b14
11317 Tallinn, Estonia
hello@eucompliancepartner.com
+33757690241

Canada

Broadview Press acknowledges the financial support of the Government of Canada for our publishing activities.

Edited by Michel Pharand
Cover design by Laura Stobbe and Aida Viziru
Book Design by Em Dash Design

Broadview Press® is the registered trademark of Broadview Press Inc.

PRINTED IN CANADA

1 2 3 4 5 6 7 8 9 10   25 26 27 28 29 30

Contents

Acknowledgements

Thanks to Stephen Latta, Archie Fields III, and everyone at Broadview Press involved in this project from its conception to the book you now hold in your hands. Thanks also to several anonymous reviewers for much helpful feedback on the road from initial proposal to final draft, and to Michel Pharand for copyediting. For the opportunity to teach the Philosophy of Leisure for their program, I am grateful to the Department of Community Development (formerly the Department of Recreation Management) at Acadia University. Lastly, thanks to the students who have taken my Philosophy of Leisure course over the years, and to anyone who derives some benefit from this book, whether in work or in leisure.

Preface

This book is intended primarily as a primary text in undergraduate courses in philosophy of leisure in recreation, leisure studies, philosophy, education, or other programs. It may also serve as a secondary text in theoretically grounded courses in recreation and leisure studies, and as an adjunct to courses in the philosophy of sport in physical education and kinesiology, including courses focusing on the nature of play and games. It should also prove a useful resource to leisure scholars and to a general readership interested in theoretical perspectives on a so-called work-life balance.

Other books on the philosophy of leisure tend to be authored works presenting an individual's unique theory or an overview of the area from generalists. The result tends to be a work that is, from a pedagogical standpoint, either deep but lacking desirable breadth or accessibility, or broad but lacking philosophical depth (since not all philosophers of leisure have an academic background in philosophy). In either case, one of two elements is missing from what would be an ideal introductory text.

In understanding leisure, other works tend to engage related, contrasting concepts such as work and recreation, while underemphasizing, in my view, the importance of close cognate concepts like play and games. Indeed, leisure and play are often characterized similarly in terms of intrinsic value (as done for their own sakes). Likewise, games form an essential part of leisure activity, and yet the foundational work on the theory of games, Bernard Suits's theory of games, is all but ignored by leisure theorists. To redress this neglect, a significant part of this work is devoted to play and games, helping us to triangulate leisure on a more complete map of the theoretical terrain. Likewise, although leisure research generally has engaged issues concerning non-Eurocentric (Asian, African, Indigenous) perspectives on leisure, the uptake among leisure philosophers has lagged, and so one chapter is devoted to those difficulties. Each chapter will be contextualized with a brief overview and followed with questions for discussion.

It is important to stress that this is a book targeting the *philosophy* of leisure specifically and not various other theoretical approaches in leisure studies.

That is, the focus here is on treatments of leisure by philosophers or other theorists whose work has philosophical significance. An interest in the methods of conceptual analysis employed by philosophers is at a premium here, rather than, say, the sociology or the psychology of leisure, except where these may pertain to philosophical questions. Empirical research methods, such as conducting surveys on what the general population's leisure experiences or concepts of leisure may be, will not be relevant to the philosophical aspects of leisure itself. As for further specifying the questions and methods in keeping with the philosophy of leisure, let this book be your guide.

It may seem paradoxical or even amusing to suggest that such a personal, sometimes frivolous thing as leisure should be subjected to serious, much less philosophical, study. It is hoped, however, that through this book students will appreciate how the significance of philosophizing about leisure mirrors that of leisure itself in revealing our need and our ability to live meaningful lives, and to step up to the ethical challenge of living a good life, one of the essential ingredients of which is leisure. The paradox here is that leisure is a realm in which we are most free and may become most human, yet we have an ethical obligation not only to include it in some form in our lives but also to ensure that doing so is a worthwhile and meaningful use of opportunities and resources. This book, naturally, will not provide such meaning, but it offers several proposals and suggestions about where and how such meaning may lie.

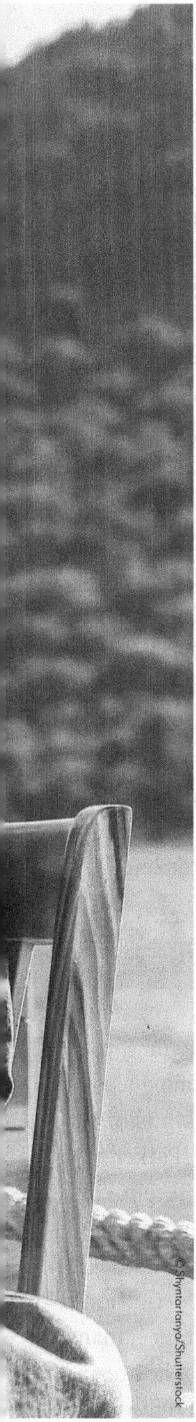

©Shyntartanya/Shutterstock

CHAPTER 1

What Is Leisure?

This chapter offers a definition of leisure based on relationships among leisure, work, recreation, and play. Since objective accounts of leisure (e.g., as free time) neglect essential normative aspects (e.g., as intrinsically valuable), leisure is defined as intrinsically motivated elective activities. This definition gives a helpful framework in which to coordinate different accounts of leisure from Aristotle to present day, to show how many such accounts emphasize certain aspects of leisure in a robust sense, and to serve as a basis for new lines of inquiry. But beyond this role, the definition may also capture, or come close to capturing, the heart of leisure itself.

INTRODUCTION

What is leisure? This question seems simple. Leisure is free time, we might say, whatever is left over after our work is done and other obligations have been met. Or, we might say, leisure is recreation, or play, not so much free time as what we fill our free time *with*. We work for the weekend, and so what we do for fun, what we choose to do on the weekend, *that's* leisure. A variety of these straightforward, unreflective answers would seem to fit the bill.

But the question is not actually that simple. Most leisure theorists agree that such answers are part of the picture, but only scratch the surface. Leisure is too deep, too complex, too important a part of human existence to be understood so superficially, especially if we are involved in scholarly inquiry in leisure studies or, more specifically, philosophy of leisure. Leisure is not just spare time, as we may choose to do extra work in our spare time. Nor is leisure well characterized negatively, as an example of "not work," for that prioritizes work instead of leisure. We work *for* the weekend and not the other way around. We don't "weekend for the work," except maybe workaholics. We might have R & R—rest and recreation—for the sake of work, and that may be leisure time in some sense, but it is not leisure in a robust sense, not leisure *itself*, which is fulfilling apart from any function, any use it might have.

In this chapter we will triangulate leisure by considering related phenomena and concepts, in particular play, recreation, and work. This analysis will foreground a definition of leisure both suggestive in itself and helping to coordinate the material in the rest of the book. Outlining how will occupy the remainder of this opening chapter after formulating the definition.

RESISTANCE TO DEFINITIONS

Before defining leisure, however, we will note two separate kinds of resistance to the notion that a theoretical term like *leisure* is one worthy of definition. In leisure studies, for instance, sometimes we are cautioned that defining leisure threatens to ignore or delegitimize differences not only in the kinds of leisure activities people choose, but in different concepts of leisure (Parker 20). What is of concern here is that there appear to be too many different concepts, covering too many different facets of leisure—as a complex cluster of phenomena—to be captured by a single definition. On the other hand, there are philosophical precedents for being suspicious of theoretical definitions. Under the influence of Ludwig Wittgenstein (1889–1951), for instance, many philosophers have considered adequate theoretical definitions of key terms to be either impossible, unnecessary, or unhelpful for doing good philosophy

(§§ 65–66). A related concern here comes from a certain stance toward the relationship between generalizations and instances: particularism is the idea that definitions should come at the end of inquiry rather than the beginning, that we should analyze different cases toward formulating a definition rather than begin with a definition (Chisholm 37).

To address these concerns, however briefly, consider the following two comments. First, with regard to the leisure theorist's concern about ignoring variety in different people's leisure concepts and preferences, suppose we characterized leisure partly in terms of freedom, that leisure consists in exercising freedom in certain ways of one's choosing. Note that what different people choose to do in exercising their freedom may vary widely and still count as exercising freedom. But we should also note that not just any concept of leisure will count equally. If my concept of leisure happens to identify it with *any* exercise of freedom, even at work or in choosing to do extra work, that does not mean that somehow work and leisure are the same thing. Choice is a part of leisure, to be sure, but motivation is part of it too. An activity such as playing a sport, which might seem to count as leisure in many cases, will not count as leisure in the case of, say, professional athletes, or amateurs who do so for health or other reasons rather than for fun.

The notion that theoretical definitions of such key terms are either impossible, unnecessary, or unhelpful, may be managed in the following way. First, even if we accept that such definitions are impossible, that does not imply that coming up with a working definition, rather than the "ultimate" definition, is a bad idea. Likewise, admitting that such definitions are not necessary for doing good philosophy does not mean they are not helpful not only in understanding the concept but also in helping to explain our intuitions about hard cases and the scope and limits of the term. The most important point, I believe, in providing a definition of leisure is that doing so will help us to coordinate various perspectives in the philosophy of leisure on the same conceptual map. Although I am optimistic that my definition of leisure captures something of its essence, I do admit that establishing its theoretical utility is, for now, a promissory note to be redeemed throughout the rest of this book in applying the framework to various philosophical perspectives on leisure.

Thus my definition of leisure is a working definition in two senses. On the one hand, it serves as a useful conceptual framework for understanding different parts of the literature and how they fit together. In this sense, it is offered as an aid to student learning rather than necessarily expressing a view of the nature of leisure itself. On the other hand, I believe my definition also captures, or comes close to capturing, the essential nature of leisure. It remains nonetheless a working definition in that I emphasize its pragmatic role in light of anti-essentialist concerns and allow for further refinements if need be. At different points in the book, one or the other role of the definition will be spotlighted. Sometimes I will assume the definition for explanatory purposes, and at other times I will show how it can be justified as an essential theory and defended from salient objections. The two roles are not entirely separate, however. The definition's theoretical utility forms part, though by no means all, of its theoretical justification. It is not only an intuitive definition, in my view, but also useful enough to be theoretically indispensable.

TRIANGULATING LEISURE

We can approach a working definition of leisure by considering similarities and differences between leisure and related concepts, particularly work, recreation, and play. To do so, we will need to draw distinctions between different kinds of motivation people may have and different kinds of activities in which people may engage.

The first important distinction is that between intrinsic and instrumental motivation. A thing has intrinsic value when it is valuable in itself, for what it is, irrespective of any use it might have. By contrast, a thing has instrumental value when it functions in a desirable way. Bitter tasting medicine has instrumental value (as a cure), but no real intrinsic value as something worth experiencing. A fun activity—think of your favourite game—by contrast, is worth experiencing in itself, and so has intrinsic value in that sense.

The second important distinction is that between elective and required activity. Some things we have to do, like go to work or school, do chores, eat and sleep. These are required activities. By contrast, things we do not have to do but choose to do, like playing games or watching TV, going for a walk, pleasure reading, these are elective activities. The model of required versus elective courses effectively represents this contrast: we have to take required courses, but may or may not choose to take certain electives. What have you done today that you had to do? That you chose to do?

Though these contrasts seem clear, they do not neatly divide activities into one or the other side of each distinction. The distinctions, in other words, are not dichotomies (where you must have one or the other of two options, but not both). An activity may have both intrinsic and instrumental value, for instance, exercising both for health and for fun. Similarly, what one does may be required, though how one does it may be elective in certain respects. Consider the difference between eating, which is necessary, and going out to a restaurant for a fine dining experience. The necessity of food becomes to some extent "leisurized" when time and money are spent, say, on a fine meal and in the company of friends.

Leisure has an objective side in that not just anything counts as leisure. This does not mean, however, that you can tell whether an activity is leisure from an objective description of it. Take the example of someone playing a sport, such as ice hockey. Is this leisure? You can't tell, at least from this bare description. Many people play hockey as a leisure activity, but some fortunate people get to play professionally. If playing hockey is your job, then it's not leisure. Likewise, if you play hockey, not because you enjoy it, but, say, for health benefits, it may count as recreation rather than leisure. Likewise, if you take the game seriously, if it's not fun for you, then for you it's not play either, even though you are still playing the game. If, however, hockey is an activity you enjoy in your spare time, it will count as leisure.

The point of this example is to illustrate how an understanding of leisure may be clarified by considering it in relation to various associated phenomena. Doing so with the conceptual apparatus of the intrinsic/instrumental distinction and the required/elective distinction will help anticipate and motivate the definition to come.

In contrast to work, leisure stands out in sharp relief. Again, *work* should be interpreted in a broad sense to include not simply gainful employment but other obligations that are not necessarily remunerative, including housework and other chores. Even social events that seem like leisure, such as parties, may count as work if they are viewed as obligations rather than opportunities. We should likewise caution against seeing all of life as dividing neatly into either work or leisure. Although there is a sense in which taking a nap might count as leisure, sleep is biologically necessary, thus a required activity, yet not really work; it is also relaxing and restorative, yet not really leisure. Work is typically instrumentally motivated, by a paycheck, for instance, rather than for the experience itself, whereas leisure is intrinsically motivated in view of activities that are enjoyable in themselves. Likewise, work is something one typically has to do, whereas leisure is where one gets to choose what one wants to do. Work can be fulfilling and freely chosen, but, unlike leisure, it need not be.

The contrast between leisure and recreation can be hard to see because the terms are often thought of as synonymous. If you take any one of your preferred pastimes, for instance, maybe your favourite sport or game, it will probably seem appropriate to categorize it either as a leisure activity or as a recreational pursuit. Pre-critically, anyway, we tend to gloss over the key distinction between descriptions of activities that are freely chosen for their own sake and those activities that are freely chosen for the sake of some further desirable end. But the difference is important. Wes Cooper puts it this way: "recreation is predominantly means-oriented—a preparation for work—whereas leisure is predominantly end-oriented; what's important to it is that it is desired for its own sake" ("Good of Leisure" 228). In these terms, recreation is meant to be restful, restorative, to help you recover for the next stretch of work, whereas leisure is valued not instrumentally but rather intrinsically. Again, amateur sports may be recreational, leisurely, or both. If one plays for sheer enjoyment, that will be leisure. If one plays for health, that will be recreation. If one plays for both reasons, participating in the sport will be both recreation and leisure.

Likely the most difficult distinction to grasp in this context is that between leisure and play, in part because *play* has two distinct senses, each of which fits—but only partly—with our concept of leisure. The first sense of *play* is what we will call the *activity* sense. Here, play is determined by a type of activity: one plays a game, or a sport, or a role in a theatrical production. Play in this sense is a close cousin of leisure because these are the kinds of activities various people often choose during leisure time. This isn't to say, of course, that all leisure activities are played. Leisure activities include watching television, going for a stroll, pleasure reading, arts and crafts, but these aren't activities we are thought of as playing. Likewise, even though sports and games are usually played as recreational or leisure activities—and, again, there is a difference there—some people play professionally. If one plays a sport or game professionally, it will not count as leisure. It can, however, also count as play in a different sense as well.

This brings us to the second sense of *play*, which is also a close cousin of leisure, specifically play in the *attitude* sense. Here, what counts as play depends, not on the type of activity in question, but on the type of mindset the participant has in engaging in an activity. The specific mindset is that of intrinsic motivation, typically enjoyment. Play in this sense is a kind of "autotelic" activity, in that its purpose (*telos*) is itself (*auto*) (Suits, "Words on Play" 117, 124). Observe that play in the attitude sense often accompanies play in the activity sense. If one plays cards for fun, that will count as play in both senses, as one is participating in a game (the activity sense) with the motive of enjoyment (the attitude sense). When this happens, when both play types coincide, play and leisure are one. But this is not always the case. The professional athlete may be deadly serious about their sport, which means that although it is still play for them in one sense (activity), it's not play in another (attitude). Also, we should note that although intrinsic motivation is most often attached to leisure activities, it might in some cases also be found in work, specifically for those fortunate enough to find their job rewarding.

That, by the way, is the source of the adage "Do what you love and you'll never work a day in your life." However, although work can be play (in the attitude, not the activity sense) if it is fulfilling, it still won't count as leisure, since it is not a freely chosen activity. The only exception here would be if a person chooses to do unnecessary work for the fun of it.

That the contrast between leisure and play is nuanced in the ways described helps to set up the definition of leisure I will propose by comparison to and with the aforementioned related terms, including *work* as antonym and the cognate terms *recreation* and *play*. The proposed definition of leisure will become clearer if we consider, again, the distinction between intrinsic and instrumental motivation, and that between required and elective activities (Table 1.1).

	Intrinsically Motivated?	**Elective Activity?**
Work	no	no
Recreation	no	yes
Play	maybe	maybe
Leisure	yes	yes

TABLE 1.1 *Comparing leisure with work, recreation, and play*

To summarize, then, work is usually instrumentally motivated and a required activity, which differs from leisure in both ways. Recreation, on the other hand, is also instrumentally motivated as refreshing us for work, and thus is like work in that respect and unlike leisure. Like leisure, however, and unlike work, recreational activities are elective rather than required. Like leisure, also, play may be intrinsically motivated and elective, but unlike leisure, play may also be instrumentally motivated and/or required, as in the case of the professional athlete. Whereas these other activities either are or may be instrumentally motivated or required, leisure stands alone.

When recreation becomes intrinsically motivated, however, it becomes leisure. Likewise, if play is both intrinsically motived and elective, it becomes leisure. In other words, our triangulation recommends a definition of leisure as *intrinsically motivated elective activities.*[1] Intrinsic motivation is not enough, nor is elective activity. Put the two together, however, and you have a twofold, more precisely a two-tier, definition of leisure. If we want to speak of chosen activities during leisure time as leisure activities, including unnecessary work

1 This definition first appeared in an earlier work (Holt, "Philosophy of Play" 132).

or other instrumentally motivated activities, that is arguably leisure, but only in a weak, watered-down sense. If such "leisure" happens to be motivated otherwise—or also—intrinsically, then it is leisure in the strong, robust, and true sense imparted by the definition.

OVERVIEW OF THE BOOK

This definition, however plausible it may be in itself, I propose not just for its inherent plausibility, as I see it, but also to provide a useful framework for coordinating a wide and diverse range of theories in the philosophy of leisure. By way of introducing the rest of the book, I will appeal explicitly to this definition in mapping the conceptual landscape. It is not that the definition itself somehow contains all that may be found in the rich tapestry of the philosophy of leisure, but rather that it may be seen as one of the threads running through the whole and helping to cohere the rest.

Aristotle and After

Undoubtedly the most towering figure in the philosophy of leisure, at least in the Western tradition, is the ancient Greek philosopher Aristotle (384–322 BCE). As Aristotle understands it, human beings are rational animals, and our happiness consists in flourishing as rational animals. This virtue is the only thing we truly value for its own sake. Animal pleasure and trivial amusements may seem to be intrinsically valued too, but that, for Aristotle, is an immature outlook. Rather, amusement is really recreation, instrumentally valuable for the sake of work. Work, too, is instrumentally valuable as a means to leisure, and leisure, at its best, consists in contemplating the nature of things. Occupying oneself with thinking about the universe is, on every level, as Aristotle sees it, superior to all forms of external, physical activity, which are less pure, depending more on external factors lying beyond one's control.

It is hard to overestimate Aristotle's seminal importance in philosophizing about leisure. This does not imply, however, a lack of significant criticisms of his view. Aristotle sees leisure at its best as somewhat passive and wholly intellectual. Beyond this limited view, however, we seem to value for its own sake contemplating not just truth but also beauty and the good, and not just contemplating but actively discovering truth, creating beauty, and cultivating relationships (Telfer 163).

The Aristotelean distinction between labour and leisure finds cultural expression much more recently in terms of different classes, in particular the wealthy leisure class. On some analyses, for instance, the leisure enjoyed by the upper classes departs from the Aristotelean ideal of intrinsic value, and leisure activities are motivated as signs of social status: one flaunts one's status through a variety of conspicuous consumption and conspicuously pointless activities (Veblen 28–29). Leisure is valued, in other words, not intrinsically but instrumentally as a sign of social standing.

Non-Western Views

Most of what we are discussing as philosophy of leisure is more precisely characterized as Western or Eurocentric philosophy of leisure. But there are other philosophical and cultural traditions, and it is somewhat unclear how well the concepts discussed so far transpose into other cultural milieus. It is important to acknowledge this limitation and say something toward addressing it. My own view, if tentative, is optimistic.

In Chinese culture, for instance, we might see little room for leisure as such in a Confucian outlook that emphasizes duty as paramount to a good life. Likewise, although meditative practice in various Buddhist traditions seems leisurely from the outside, the achievement of enlightenment is a task of great difficulty and urgency to avoid life's suffering. More promising, however, is Taoism, in which we find an analogue of the Western concept of leisure in *hsiao yao*, grounded in the principle of *wu-wei* ("no-action"), including purposes of self-cultivation and freedom from necessity (Yeh and Chick 1, 9). Indeed, Taoism lies at the root of various leisure activities in the Chinese tradition (Wang and Stringer 33). The principle of living in accordance with nature, which we find in Taoism, we also find in different perspectives in the Western tradition, including Epicureanism and notably Stoicism. Such parallels stress the importance of cross-cultural analysis for leisure studies generally and for the philosophy of leisure specifically.

Understanding leisure in Indigenous cultures will be difficult irrespective of whether relevant languages appear to have or to lack words for leisure. The Hawaiian *manawa nanea*, for instance, is sometimes taken to indicate leisure, yet literally means "lying in a shallow lagoon with water flowing over you while birds are singing" (Fox 404). An idiomatic interpretation appears to ignore important layers and subtleties of meaning. Colonial perspectives often yield simplistic reduction of traditional leisure activities to wasting time or "mere celebration" (Naidoo 94). The presumption in some cases seems to be that leisure should be of a certain sort with a certain sort of accompanying attitude, but this betrays both a lack of sensitivity to cross-cultural varieties in what activities are valued, and why, and how in many Indigenous cultures there are closer ties between individual and social value than a superficial

Eurocentric view might tolerate. The extension of Eurocentric concepts of leisure to other cultures, then, must be both tentative and sensitive, provisional and respectful. The extent to which this is feasible, in some cases perhaps more than in others, will remain a matter of some debate.

Time for Reflection

Thinking of leisure as free time is understandable, since it captures the contrast between leisure and obligatory activity. But this respects only the "elective activities" part of our definition of leisure, not the "intrinsically motivated" part. The results are limiting, and not just because we tend to conceive leisure in a negative sense, as freedom *from* work. Even if we conceive leisure positively, as freedom *to* engage in chosen activities, our modern concept of time, and of free time, disposes us to accept a corresponding quantitative rather than qualitative view of leisure (Goodale and Godbey 138), of *how much* time we have rather than *how good* our free-time activities are. Such commodification of time, and by extension leisure, has its perils.

Such perils include seeing ourselves too much or essentially as productive workers or active consumers. To the extent that work defines us, what we do in leisure time doesn't really matter, so long as it restores us for work. Too much free time will be seen as idleness and sloth unless we use it for productive activities. Josef Pieper (1904–97) resists this characterization of leisure. For Pieper, however, a lack of purpose induces not idleness but a kind of despairing restlessness, a lack of true leisure. By contrast, we witness true leisure especially in appropriate celebrations, feasts, and festivals, in which we not only enjoy the fruits of our labour but affirm existence itself along with our place in it (Pieper 48–99). If we likewise see ourselves too much as leisure consumers, that will result in shallow and unreflective instead of authentic leisure choices (Ramsay 31–32). Leisure gives us opportunities, against such reductive accounts, to explore, express, and be ourselves.

Play and Games

The notion of leisure as a means of self-expression and self-discovery brings us back to the affinities between leisure and play. Indeed, where Pieper views leisure as the basis of culture, Johan Huizinga (1872–1945) assigns that role to play.[2] In a way that dovetails with our twofold definition of leisure, Huizinga stresses the importance of play as standing apart from everyday life (similar

2 Huizinga's book *Homo Ludens* (1938) is subtitled *A Study of the Play-Element in Culture.*

to the elective activities of leisure) and as being done for its own sake (like leisure). As Huizinga sees it, even in the most serious parts of culture, where it might be difficult to discern, there will always be an element of play. Other theorists, similarly, see our natural inclination to play as expressing itself sometimes in work, if it is creative rather than drudgery, as well as leisure (Nash 82). We may judge the quality of work and leisure alike by how well either rewards our active engagement as creative beings.

Play does not always involve participation in games, but it often does, and games are one of the dominant expressions of our inclination to play. A classic philosophical account of games is given by Bernard Suits (1925–2007). In games, we accept the arbitrary constraints of rules in a way that we wouldn't in everyday life, because it is the rules that define games we want to play. Hence, for Suits, playing a game is "the voluntary attempt to overcome unnecessary obstacles"; such game-play is so central to Suits's view of human happiness that he believes it would become the principal activity in an ideal world (*Grasshopper* 55, 154). Suits presents this type of leisure as happiness itself.

Freedom and Authenticity

Although we are far from living in such a utopia, the freedom required for such leisure is a vital part of the types of leisure we may enjoy in real life. But there is a tension here between a commitment to individual freedom in leisure and the fact that many people seem to make bad choices in leisure activities, opting for lower pleasures of amusement and distraction rather than higher pleasures of the sort more appropriate for human beings (though there will be different views on what counts as a higher or lower pleasure) (Charles 50–51). This tension emphasizes the place of leisure education, although the extent to which leisure is good will nonetheless depend on an individual's own unique, current, self-directed, end-oriented preferences (Cooper, "Good of Leisure" 227).

Our definition of leisure as intrinsically motivated elective *activities* may appear to fit badly with varieties of leisure as idleness. Some theorists see idleness as sloth or laziness, which is a kind of vice, a bad character trait. As Cooper puts it, "there is a difference between leisure and idleness, mere freedom from obligation.... there is something personally rewarding in leisure, whereas leisure as idleness may be boring and stultifying" ("Good of Leisure" 227). Others, however, see idleness as a crucial and neglected part of leisure including more passive, less demanding, enjoyable activities. Take, for example, the title of Bertrand Russell's (1872–1970) famous apology for leisure, "In Praise of Idleness." We might even interpret Aristotle's notion of the ideal form of leisure, contemplation, as a blending of leisure as idleness, since it is not physically active, and leisure as activity, since it is intellectually active and so not purely passive.

Whatever our individual leisure preferences, though, whether on the active or passive side or some of both, it would seem important that we make such choices authentically, that we be true to ourselves not only generally in life but specifically in leisure, since we will have a wider degree of freedom there than when obligations are in effect. This will depend partly on individuals themselves and partly on the situations, material and social, they inhabit. Choosing a certain form of leisure as a status symbol à la Veblen—that is, for instrumental rather than intrinsic reasons—will inevitably seem inauthentic, whereas choosing leisure activities for intrinsic reasons irrespective of others' opinions will have a better claim to authenticity (Coe 95, 98). Although social structures may severely limit or eliminate the scope of meaningful choices available to us (Carr 148), we may still hope for authentic, personal enlightenment through exercising freedom, if nowhere else, in our leisure choices.

QUESTIONS FOR CONSIDERATION

- Are there concepts besides work, recreation, and play that help inform our concept of leisure?
- Which, if either, seems more important to you, and why: that an activity is intrinsically motivated or that it is freely chosen?
- Is the twofold definition of leisure too demanding? Are there contexts in which it makes sense to equate leisure with free time?
- Are there essential aspects of leisure excluded from the proposed definition?
- Which of the above approaches to the philosophy of leisure do you find the most insightful? Why?
- Which of the above approaches to the philosophy of leisure do you find the least insightful? Why?

© LightField Studios/Shutterstock

CHAPTER 2

Aristotle on Leisure

The focus of this chapter is the highly influential account of leisure offered by Aristotle some two and a half millennia ago. Aristotle sees human happiness as a matter of eudaimonia, *of the soul being in a good state. Such a good state requires virtue, and in leisure we express our highest virtue as human beings, which for Aristotle is seen in intellectual contemplation rather than action. After discussing a handful of objections to Aristotle's view, we will look at other ancient views among which Aristotle's stands out in sharp relief.*

INTRODUCTION

Many of us tend to think of happiness and leisure in terms of achieving a work-life balance. We may try to explain certain problems in terms of an imbalance between the two, where either work or life is too dominant and leaves insufficient room for the other.[1] We may think that someone is unhappy because they work too hard, or that someone else has too much leisure, lacks purpose, and doesn't work hard enough. The solution in both cases, like the problem, is quantitative: reduce the excessive work (or leisure) and increase the corresponding leisure (or work) accordingly. The more a work-life balance is achieved, the happier the person in question will be.

As we shall see, this way of thinking about leisure does not sit well with Aristotle's account of happiness and what it means to live a good life. The problem for Aristotle is that we should see work and leisure not quantitatively, not as counterparts, but rather qualitatively, in terms of which has more value. For Aristotle there is no question: leisure has greater value—a more important kind of value—than work. Not all types of leisure count the same, either. Just as leisure and work occupy different levels in a hierarchy of values, so too do different types of leisure. The intuitive difference between more and less fulfilling work is mirrored by Aristotle's view that there is a crucial difference between more and less worthwhile and fulfilling leisure. Having a work-life imbalance may mean lacking, not a certain *amount* of leisure, but a certain *kind* of leisure. No wonder leisure theorists who think our culture has gone astray often urge us to reclaim an Aristotelean outlook on leisure.[2]

HUMAN FLOURISHING

Suppose that being happy requires, or perhaps simply amounts to, living well, to living as one ought to as a human being. This certainly holds for Aristotle. Living a good life, in Aristotle's view, means being in a state of *eudaimonia*, of one's soul (*daimon*) being in a good (*eu*) state of order. Where we, in a more modern frame of mind, tend to see living well in terms of "getting yourself together" and being *productive*, such a work ethic is at odds with Aristotle's view. According to Aristotle, living well is rooted not in a work ethic but in a virtue ethic. Virtues are positive character traits such as wisdom and courage, and it is having and honing these, rather than being productive, that makes

1 The phrase *work-life balance* curiously implies that work is not a part of life but something apart from it.

2 See for example de Grazia (332) and Ramsay (43), among others.

one happy, that makes one flourish, as a human being. Though Aristotle understands that learning virtue implies effort, the crown jewel in his account of the good life is reserved, not for the work of learning virtue but rather for the leisure of expressing virtue in certain ways.

Virtue is what places human beings above mere animals but below the gods in the hierarchy of being. We are animals, but *rational* animals, so in the hierarchy of being we rank above the "mere brutish" realm of nonhuman animals but below the superhuman realm of the divine, pure rationality of the gods. In learning virtue, we ascend a human hierarchy from a state just above brutishness to a state just below divinity. We learn virtue by developing the right habits (Aristotle 23). Before we do so, however, we may fail in several ways. We may exhibit vice, where vice is as a negative character trait (e.g., cowardice) indicating a lack of virtue (e.g., courage). Such a state nonetheless ranks above mere brutishness because the potential for learning virtue is present, though latent. Try thinking of it in terms of the metaphor of climbing a ladder, rung by rung, from vice into virtue. One learns first to want to do the right thing even though one's will is too weak to do it (*akrasia*). Then, one learns self-control and is able to do the right thing even though one is inclined to do the wrong thing. Lastly, as doing the right thing becomes a habit, one is naturally inclined and pleasurably disposed to doing the right thing when the situation demands it, such as being courageous in wartime.

The heart of Aristotle's account of virtue is evoked by the phrase *doctrine of the mean*, and is developed in the *Nicomachean Ethics* (and particularly bk. 2). The word *mean* here should suggest an intermediate state between opposite extremes. These opposite extremes, for Aristotle, are both vices: one of deficit, of not having enough of the virtue, the other of excess, of having too much of the virtue, with virtue in between. A person has courage when they occupy an intermediate state between cowardice and rashness or foolhardiness. When courage is called for, they don't run away from the danger, nor do they impetuously confront the danger. A person exhibits moderation in their tastes by avoiding self-denial (asceticism) on one side and self-indulgence (hedonism) on the other. A person exhibits justice by avoiding both leniency and cruelty, by giving people neither more nor less than they deserve. Virtue thus has a rational aspect, and as far as leisure is concerned, it is for Aristotle, as we shall see, the best expression of our highest virtue, and this is to be understood in terms of quality rather than quantity.

As already noted, the way we think about a work-life balance doesn't fit well with Aristotle's view of leisure, since it implies a quantitative rather than qualitative perspective on human activities. We will now turn to the heart of Aristotle's account of leisure—the best kind of leisure for a human being—by contrasting leisure with work on the one hand, amusement on the other, and by grasping Aristotle's view that leisure activities come in different grades of quality, and that the very best kind of leisure is that which is most distinctively, most properly human.

Note first the rather obvious distinction between work and leisure. For Aristotle, intuitively, both work and leisure are important, but for different reasons. Although a "happy life is thought to be virtuous," and "a virtuous life requires exertion" (193), the value of work does not lie in exertion but in providing us with "the necessaries of life" (194). We work and take care of other obligations for the sake of leisure, which has intrinsic value, that is, is valued in itself, for what it is rather than for what it does. As Aristotle puts it, "we are busy that we may have leisure" (195). This isn't to say that leisure activities have no instrumental value period. Walking, for instance, might be enjoyable and also have health benefits. But what makes an activity like walking leisurely rather than work or work-like is its being valued for what it is rather than what it does. If walking becomes more of a health compulsion than an enjoyable activity, it has become more work-like than leisurely.

THE BEST LEISURE

When Aristotle says "we are busy that we may have leisure," he has in mind a significant difference between activities that are not free but forced, not relaxed but busy (think of *business* as deriving from *busy-ness*). The intrinsic value of leisure, as something valued for its own sake, is contrasted with the instrumental value of these busy activities, which are valued as means to relaxed, leisurely activities. If we are busy that we may have leisure, then, for Aristotle we would not be busy, doing work and chores, if we didn't have to, if our leisure didn't so often depend on it. The implied ideal, impractical as it is for most people, would be a life of leisure.

The idea that human happiness is related to leisure is intuitive, but Aristotle's commitment is stronger—that happiness actually depends on leisure. When we think of people at their happiest, often what comes to mind is a leisure scenario: relaxing, recreating, vacationing. When we think of people unhappy or less happy, we might imagine them doing things not chosen but required: work, chores, or other necessary things (e.g., court appearances). This leaves us with the misleading sense that leisure consists in fun activities. Indeed, we often picture leisure as amusement and recreation. But, as we will see, according to Aristotle, leisure stands apart from amusement or recreation.

Not all activities that fit this relaxed, enjoyable profile would, for Aristotle, count as leisure. Suppose you are in the middle of a hard week and look forward to decompressing on the weekend. Maybe you have specific plans to go out with friends and blow off some steam, take a self-care day, or binge-watch some guilty pleasure. As enjoyable as these activities may be, in Aristotle's view the more they are valued as ways to recharge, to recover for the following week, the more they count, not as true leisure, but as amusement or recreation. Aristotle puts it this way:

> Happiness, therefore, does not lie in amusement; it would, indeed, be strange if the end were amusement, and one were to take trouble and suffer hardship all one's life in order to amuse oneself.... Now to exert oneself and work for the sake of amusement seems silly and utterly childish. But to amuse oneself in order that one may exert oneself ... seems right; for amusement is a sort of relaxation, and we need relaxation because we cannot work continuously. Relaxation, then, is not an end; for it is taken for the sake of activity. (193)

Where work and chores are instrumentally valuable as a means to leisure, the value of recreation—enjoyable or not—lies in its restorative nature. Work gives importance to recreation, just as leisure gives importance to work.

What, then, counts as leisure for Aristotle? True leisure, or the best leisure, for Aristotle, is *pure* leisure. It is not just valued for its own sake, it is also *not* valued instrumentally. You may think that, all else being equal, an activity that has a certain intrinsic value but no extra instrumental value would be inferior to an activity with the same intrinsic value *along with* instrumental value besides.[3] If you enjoy a certain kind of physical exercise that is also good for your health, that would be better than an equally enjoyable activity without such additional benefits. But what Aristotle holds as true leisure or the best sort of leisure will be some activity valued intrinsically but not instrumentally, for it will be leisure in its purest form and as reflecting the best in our essential nature as human beings.

So the best leisure, according to Aristotle, will be the form that best fits our essential nature as rational beings. He holds this to be nothing other than contemplation, intellectual contemplation, thinking about the nature of things. Why? Because "this activity alone would seem to be loved for its own sake" (194). Again, to be clear, although there are many other activities loved for their own sake, they are also loved for other, less pure reasons. For Aristotle, then, it is the mindset of a philosopher's thinking deeply about

---

3 See Cooper ("Leisure Theory" 6) on the contrast between Aristotle's and Plato's views here. On the latter, instrumental value is seen as potentially adding to rather than detracting from leisure's value.

the nature of reality, considering truth, goodness, and beauty, that best illustrates and is indeed the best form of leisure. This makes the philosopher not only "the dearest to the gods" but also "the happiest" for being as close to the divine as is possible for humans (198). Make no mistake. Aristotle does not praise *doing* philosophy so much as *thinking* philosophically. His praise is not for teaching philosophy or writing philosophy—for those are "busy" actions—but rather for considering the world in that way, as a philosopher does. More leisurely and more philosophical than me *writing* this book is you *reading* it, not because you have to but because you choose to, prompting your own philosophical reflections on the nature of leisure.

To take another example, consider your favourite sport (if you have one, or imagine someone else's as your own). Suppose you enjoy playing the sport, watching it played by others, and thinking about it as a connoisseur of the game. Suppose all three count as leisure activities in that you aren't a professional athlete, pundit, or philosopher of sport. Having experience playing the game yourself may enrich your viewing and connoisseurship. But, for Aristotle, the least leisurely of these activities is playing the sport yourself, in part because of instrumental benefits such as better health and opportunities to socialize. Watching the sport will count as more leisurely and of lesser instrumental benefit, perhaps as amusement. But thinking about the sport, what you like about it, what you know about it, what it suggests about human nature, and so forth, that will count as the most leisurely, an example of pure leisure valued for its own sake.

What this points to in Aristotle's view is a key distinction between *contemplation* and *action* as different forms of leisure, with contemplation held as the superior form. Why does Aristotle take contemplative forms to be superior to more active forms? Here are the reasons, some interrelated, others apparently not (194–95):

1. Contemplation engages the best within us as human beings, the intellect unencumbered by practical concerns. Action, on the other hand, is more focused, and engages practical rather than pure reason.

2. Contemplation concerns not only the best in us but also the best object, truth, the nature of reality, whereas action concerns lesser, specific objects and purposes. Where contemplation is on a grand scale, action is necessarily on a smaller, more idiosyncratic scale.

3. Contemplation is the most self-sufficient of human activities, with virtually no requirements of other people, special equipment, individual

power, goods, or occasions. Action is far less self-sufficient, often with significant requirements of others, equipment, power, goods, and occasions.

4. As an activity, contemplation is the most continuous, feasible for sustained periods of time without fatigue or loss of interest. Action, by contrast, is invariably much more sporadic and fatiguing, and one is apt to lose interest in it rather quickly.

5. Similarly, the pleasures of contemplation are lasting and relatively pure, whereas those of action tend to be short-lived and mixed, requiring unpleasant aspects of effort, discomfort, anxiousness, pain, and so forth.

6. Contemplation is an end in itself, whereas action, even if intrinsically valued, is inevitably a means to some further end and is thus subject to instrumental concerns. This helps explain the difference between the two in terms of pleasure profiles.

7. Contemplation is the most divine of human activities, giving us a glimpse of, and to a certain extent a share in, what it is like to be a god. Action, however, is not divine in any degree, and remains merely human.[4]

For these reasons, in Aristotle's view contemplation is held to be the best kind of leisure and to that extent the best representation of what leisure can be. Contemplation is hence in both senses of the term the *paradigm* of Aristotelean leisure. But what of the other, more active forms of leisure held to be, in various respects mentioned above, inferior? Addressing active leisure will be deferred until the next section where it arises naturally in the context of criticisms of the Aristotelean account of leisure.

CRITICISMS OF ARISTOTLE

Among various criticisms of Aristotle's view, we will focus on those that take issue with his paradigm of leisure specifically and with the context in which Aristotle developed his theory. The first reflects a concern that Aristotle's notion of the scope of leisure is too narrow and thus misleading by excluding

4 Aristotle has the pantheon of ancient Greek gods—Zeus and company—in mind here. It isn't that gods never act, but rather that unlike us they never have to. When they do, they are at their most humanlike, just as when we contemplate, we are at our most godlike.

or undervaluing certain kinds of leisure. The second reflects a concern with the kind of society that is presupposed by Aristotle's view and to which it is meant to apply.

Taking the contemplation of eternal truths to be the paradigm of leisure seems to be unduly narrow in scope. As Telfer puts it, we may "feel there are things worthy of contemplation other than Aristotle's necessary truths, such as great works of art and the wonders and beauties of nature"; but even this expanded notion of worthy things to contemplate leaves us with a "time to stop and stare" model that is "unsatisfactorily *passive*" (158). Leisure activities seem to include more energetic, fun activities along with more contemplative, relaxing ones. But, according to Aristotle, as action occurs in the realm of practical virtues, and since "the activity of the practical virtues is exhibited in political or military affairs ... the actions concerned with these seem to be unleisurely" (195). In other words, fun activities exercise practical virtues, and so they retain some of the unleisurely quality of practical affairs. In the extreme, then, Aristotle's view seems to exclude actions altogether from the category of leisure. The only true leisure activities would be contemplative, not active.

There are reasons, however, to resist such a narrow reading of Aristotle's view, to include some actions as examples, if lesser examples, of Aristotelean leisure. If we pivot from what Aristotle says in the *Nicomachean Ethics* to what he says elsewhere (i.e., the *Politics*), we will include among leisure activities in a civil society certain ways of relating with one another (Hemingway 189). Think of socializing with friends or going to the theatre, for instance. These will count as leisure activities, at least in some sense. They are freely chosen and enjoyable in themselves. They may count lower than contemplation on the scale of leisure quality, since they are less self-sustainable and may have instrumental value as well, but that doesn't imply that they aren't important leisure activities, much less leisure at all, for Aristotle. Indeed, Aristotle sees human beings not only as rational animals but as political animals. Part of what it means to be a human being is to exist and function with others in civil society. He stresses the importance for human beings in civil society of such social interactions as friendship (in the *Politics*) and theatregoing (in the *Poetics*). More active, less self-sustaining forms of leisure arguably still count as important forms, if not the highest form, of Aristotelean leisure.

A related concern is that Aristotle's distinction between action and contemplation, although reasonable, seems to be a false dichotomy. Contemplation is a kind of activity, even though a rather passive and inactive one. But the real issue is the sense that contemplation and action are held to be mutually exclusive: if one is contemplating, one is inactive, and if one is active, whatever happens in one's mind, it is at most practically focused rather than contemplative mental activity. If we consider Asian culture here, we might contrast our mental image of a shaolin monk sitting in meditation with the image of that same person practising kung fu. Where our Western understanding tends to think of such activities as entirely distinct, Eastern views often see such practices as overlapping. It is not unusual, for instance, for practising choreographed forms in martial arts to be considered a form of "moving meditation" (Cook 57). We might also observe that, for some people, certain basic physical tasks may similarly free the mind for more meditative musings. It is not unusual for someone doing the dishes or other chores to do so meditatively. In this sense, although contemplation need not be active, it need not be inactive either, a potential problem for Aristotle's view. Certain actions appear not just to facilitate contemplation but to be contemplative in themselves.

Another objection arises if we consider that Aristotle's cultural context is, in certain crucial respects, radically different from our own. Aristotle lived at a time when slavery was both common and widely accepted. "Athenian slave-owners, for instance, employed part of their leisure in making a permanent contribution to civilisation which would have been impossible under a just economic system" (B. Russell 5). Aristotle's theory of leisure presupposes an unjust society built on the labour of slaves and relegating to subordinate status women and labourers, with members of these groups excluded from the free citizenry who may fully enjoy leisure. So pictured, what we should regard as a fundamentally flawed society may appear to have little to tell us about leisure. That said, however, nothing prevents us, from our contemporary point of view, understanding leisure in Aristotle's sense as being properly available to everyone.

To dismiss altogether Aristotle's account of leisure because it arose in a morally problematic cultural context is to commit the genetic fallacy: the mistake of believing the properties of a thing to be determined by the properties of its origin. Note, by the way, that our own culture may be morally problematic—in ways we have yet to discover—as well, but that does not necessarily invalidate our perspective on moral matters. We would also be guilty of a fallacy if we were to disregard Aristotle's view as irrelevant simply because it's 2,500 years old, or because originally it was meant to apply to city-states like ancient Athens rather than nation-states like modern Greece. Despite the substantial cultural distance between Aristotle's time and ours, that in no way indicates that his view of leisure is somehow irrelevant. Indeed, as we will see in subsequent chapters, contemporary leisure may be seen as impoverished by neglecting an Aristotle-style approach to leisure.

OTHER ANCIENT VIEWS

Though Aristotle's theory stands preeminent in Western culture among ancient views of leisure, it is by no means the only view. Indeed, our understanding of Aristotle may be enhanced by considering the wider cultural context, specifically some of his philosophical predecessors and successors.

One of Aristotle's predecessors is Socrates, who is arguably the ultimate exemplar of living life philosophically. Socrates is known not for writing philosophy but for talking philosophy with his fellow citizens in ancient Athens, talking about the ultimate nature of reality and what it means to live a good life. These conversations occurred typically in decidedly *leisure* contexts: taking a walk, a chance meeting after a public event, relaxing after food and drink at a party. This picture of Socrates as a philosopher at leisure, or more precisely, as using leisure to do philosophy, comes from a series of dialogues written by his student, Plato, another great philosopher who in turn taught Aristotle. In Plato's *Symposium*, for instance, Socrates engages various fellow citizens at a party in discussing the nature of love. This image of the philosopher at leisure, teaching and learning through conversation, provides an interesting complement to Aristotelean leisure as isolated contemplation. Both forms of philosophizing would seem, to the ancient mind, to be excellent uses of leisure, and to potentially be of mutual benefit, each enriching the other.

Successors to Aristotle in the ancient world, both Greek and Roman, reflect his view in some respects and depart from it in others. The Cynics, for instance, similarly stressed a detachment from material goods and pleasures, but they looked more favourably on the pleasure and leisure enjoyed by non-human animals: "[i]n some ways theirs was a back to nature movement; not fleeing the cities but living in an almost primitive way" (Goodale and Godbey 25). The Epicureans likewise embraced sensual pleasures, at least in moderation, but like Aristotle held intellectual pleasures to be superior (Goodale and Godbey 26).

The Stoics likewise embraced moderation, urging us not to force pleasure to come or to be anxious when it eludes us—because that is beyond our control—but to partake of it when it comes, since that is rational. Indeed, for the Stoics it is not just human beings but the universe itself that is rational, and our task is to align our own intelligence with that of the universe. This task implies not only doing our duty in work but, as Seneca asserts in an Aristotelean vein (218), leaves ample room for contemplative leisure.

But these remarks barely hint at the cultural legacy of Aristotle's view of leisure. In the next chapter we will begin to appreciate the enormous scope of this legacy, in both positive and negative respects, in greater detail.

QUESTIONS FOR CONSIDERATION

- How well do your favourite leisure activities fit—or fail to fit—Aristotle's view?
- Does Aristotle overestimate leisure's rational/contemplative side? Is he right that humans are *rational* animals?
- Why does Aristotle undervalue non-intellectual leisure?
- Why is *thinking* about truth better leisure than *pursuing* truth?
- What besides truth is worth contemplating, and how does contemplation differ from, say, daydreaming?
- How does Aristotle's view of contemplative leisure fit with the idea that one should be free to *choose* one's leisure?

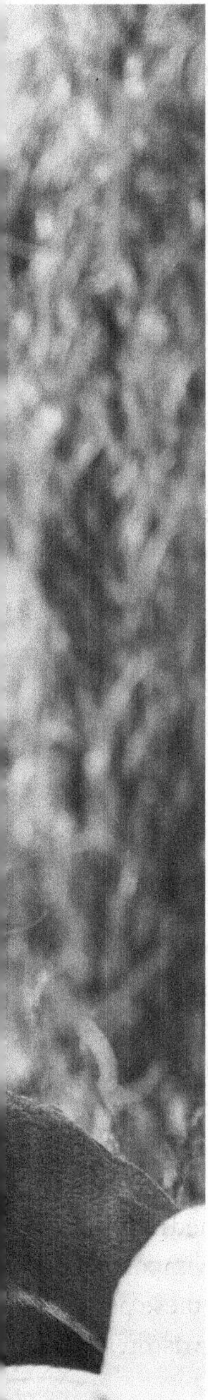

CHAPTER 3

In Aristotle's Wake

This chapter explores Aristotle's cultural legacy not only in theorizing about leisure and what is the best use of leisure, but in deep-seated distinctions in how we understand different types of education (liberal arts versus vocational school) and different social classes (the leisure class as marked by a self-assertive, conspicuous leisure signifying its status). Despite the unfortunate aspects of this legacy, however, there continue to be calls to revive the Aristotelean perspective on leisure as an antidote to inadequate ordinary and instrumental views of leisure, often with a more inclusive sense of worthy leisure activities and a more democratic sense of who should enjoy them.

INTRODUCTION

It would be hard to overstate the importance of Aristotle's thought in the history of Western culture. His system of reasoning based on interrelationships among categories—categorical logic—was the standard for over 2,000 years. His ethics, in which good actions are explained as deriving from virtues, the positive character traits learned from moral exemplars, provides the basis for contemporary virtue ethics, one of only a handful of moral theories that have retained currency since their inception, and the oldest among such theories. Although flawed by current standards, Aristotle's account of the sciences remained unsurpassed until the early modern period. But impressive as these résumé entries may be, they are but highlights of an indelible intellectual legacy, only part of which concerns us here.

That part, of course, is Aristotle's view of leisure and of the society in which, at its best, it is held up as the crowning part, the very best of human activities. In tracing this part of Aristotle's legacy, I will focus on three distinct but related topics: broadening Aristotle's account of worthy leisure activities, the educational implications of Aristotle's distinction between labour and leisure, and the fundamental class distinction that, despite having evolved into different iterations since ancient times, remains to this day.

A+ LEISURE

One modern leisure philosopher following in Aristotle's wake is Elizabeth Telfer. She takes the lead from Aristotle's view in bridging from ordinary, pre-reflective, and reductively instrumental concepts of leisure to a view which like Aristotle's is rooted in intrinsic value, but unlike Aristotle's takes a much wider view both of objects worthy of contemplation and what activities may count as both intrinsically worthy and leisurely besides contemplation. Because Telfer's account explicitly expands on Aristotle's in these two distinct but complementary ways, I find it useful to label her view "Aristotle plus" or simply "A+" leisure. Like Aristotle, Telfer is concerned not just with which activities may constitute leisure but also, and more importantly, with which activities are worthy of leisurely pursuit. Despite these parallels, Telfer's view is motivated in part by a critical take on her Aristotelean inspiration.

In Telfer's view, both our ordinary concept of leisure and an instrumental concept of leisure are misguided and misguiding, the former for generating various problems of leisure, the latter for giving us inadequate and confused solutions to such problems. Our everyday concept of leisure, in Telfer's words, is "that time which a person can use as he chooses, which is free from necessity and obligation" (152). In this formulation, leisure is contrasted not only with work (as gainful employment) but also with meeting biological needs and doing chores. The emphasis here is on the elective nature of leisure activities, those we freely choose, rather than what motivates or is valuable about them. This everyday notion of leisure is inadequate, for Telfer, because it leaves unanswered key questions. What, for instance, is the proper place of leisure in life? What leisure training is appropriate, and for whom? How much leisure is optimal, and what kinds? To what extent are we entitled to leisure? The ordinary concept of leisure harbours an implicit tension between the sense that there are, objectively, better and worse forms of leisure and the sense that we are under no obligation to choose those forms that are better.

One good thing about the ordinary concept as articulated by Telfer is the sense that leisure in a robust sense is attitude-dependent and, perhaps unexpectedly, that non-leisure activities may be partly leisurized. Consider first the activity of visiting your family on the weekend. Is this leisure? Well, that it is a weekend activity will certainly suggest as much, and it seems that, objectively speaking, it is an elective activity. However, to the extent that you see the visit as an obligation, as something you have to do, it is not a leisure activity. The notion of partial leisurization becomes clearer if we consider not just meeting biological needs, but doing more, in doing so, than is strictly necessary. We need to eat, of course, but the more time, money, or effort we put into meeting that need beyond necessity—enjoying haute cuisine at a restaurant or preparing a special meal at home—the more we have leisurized it.

Even so, the basic value of such necessary activities aligns with work and so suggests a reductive account of leisure as having chiefly instrumental value in helping us be productive at work and therefore maximizing our contribution to society. Think of such a reductive view as essentially turning leisure into recreation, or seeing the latter as the heart of the former. On this view, the amount and type of leisure one should have and whatever leisure education may be required for it, are functions purely of the type of work one has. For instance, those with more physically demanding jobs should, on this view, probably have more relaxing and restorative forms of leisure than those with more sedentary jobs who would be better off with more physically active forms of leisure. Whatever its merits, however, Telfer is clear that this view confuses employment with productivity, insisting that leisure itself, even worthwhile leisure or the best kind of leisure, can be productive, in some ways more so than employment (158–59). Consider, for example, that the poet T.S. Eliot had a day job as a bank clerk, which, though necessary, certainly pales in comparison with his cultural contributions as a writer. Taking a step back, in contrast to unproductive recreational amusement, meaningful leisure may indeed be productive, if not strictly useful, and thus is similar in a twofold sense to voluntary as opposed to obligatory work.

To overcome both the ordinary and the instrumentally reductive views of leisure, Telfer appeals to Aristotle, whose view is already familiar, stressing the intrinsic value of the intellectual contemplation of truth. We assume the elective dimension of leisure here but stress the importance of intrinsic value in such activities for characterizing what leisure, in a robust sense, is and ought to be. Recall, however, that Telfer criticizes Aristotle's account as a "stop and stare" model of leisure that is both too limited and too passive, not that contemplating truth doesn't, but rather that other activities will also, count among the best forms of leisure. According to Telfer, there are objects of contemplation no less worthy than truth, and more active forms of leisure no less worthy than contemplation.

In considering the potential scope of intellectual contemplation, it would seem that, in addition to truth, one worthy contemplable is beauty. Truth might itself be considered beautiful, but so too are "great works of art and the wonders and beauty of Nature" (Telfer 158). In addition to what Telfer explicitly mentions here, we might consider not just truth and beauty but also *the good* (in a moral sense) to be worthy of contemplation, and in nature *the sublime*, where we are overwhelmed by something either vast, such as the clear night sky, or fearsome, such as a ferocious storm when we are safely indoors. As much as Telfer seeks to broaden the scope of worthy contemplables, then, we might consider the possibility of widening it still further. One might attribute to Aristotle himself such a wide interpretation of contemplation-worthy objects. Perhaps, for instance, truth includes both the beautiful and the good, and perhaps the beautiful subsumes the sublime. But that is not how either Aristotle or these terms are customarily interpreted.

As already mentioned, however, Telfer seeks to broaden the scope of leisure, of the best leisure, in another, decidedly anti-Aristotelean way. Where Aristotle insists that the best leisure is contemplative rather than active, Telfer wishes to include certain active forms of it in the category of best leisure also. If we think of contemplating truth or beauty as intrinsically valuable, for instance, we should also see the *discovery* of truth by doing science and the *creation* of beauty by doing art as no less worthy, as valuable in themselves irrespective of possible results (158–59). Likewise, Telfer sees Aristotle as giving short shrift to friendships as valued for their own sake and as marginalizing from the intrinsic value of leisure activity broadly construed the *enjoyment* of such activity by the subject (159). But as we saw in the last chapter, Aristotle does seem to include relating with friends among leisure activities, even if these count as lesser forms than contemplation. In discussing contemplation specifically, likewise, Aristotle doesn't shy away from descriptions in which intrinsic value and pleasure quality are intimately connected.

We might similarly seek a more expansive account not by enlarging the scope of what is worth contemplating or by adding activities besides contemplation to the list of "best leisure," but by adopting a wider view of activities that may count as contemplative, as we saw in the previous chapter. Similarly, consider Holba's proposal that communicative practices such as conversation can be infused with and enriched by contemplative or philosophical leisure (81). As conversation may be little more than mere chatter or idle talk, it may also be elevated and preserved as an artform. Maintaining conversation as an art, for Holba, depends on keeping in regular touch with contemplative leisure. Thus artful conversation may itself be philosophical, or at any rate sustained by those who are as conversant with contemplation as they are with one another.

Telfer's critique and expansion of Aristotle's view points to an important distinction between a subjective and an objective understanding of intrinsic value, of valuing some activity for its own sake. If leisure is defined as intrinsically motivated elective activities (see Chapter 1), this leaves open whether such intrinsic motivation lies in the subject's participatory pleasure or—additionally or alternatively—in their assessment of an activity's objective value. You might think of volunteering for a charity as worthy irrespective of enjoyment. By the same token, you may find fun certain activities that are questionable or neutral (grey leisure) or even immoral or criminal (dark leisure). Note that although Telfer considers Aristotle to have marginalized pleasure in his account, she emphasizes rather the more objective sense of intrinsic value when affirming that "the more leisure the better, provided people are able to fill it with worthwhile activities" (160) as well as that "[w]e can value ... useful lives for their own sakes" (162), with work itself not necessarily being pointless apart from results, acknowledging at least a partial work ethic. That our definition of leisure is flexible enough to incorporate both senses of intrinsic value—subjective and objective—counts as a theoretical strength.

Against Telfer's attempt to broaden Aristotle's view into A+ leisure, one might counter that what Aristotle says about the purity of intellectual contemplation of truth still holds. Might the beauties of art or nature simply be subsumed under the rubric of contemplating truth? Or else might they be relegated as inferior objects of contemplation as relatively short-lived and too closely tied to biological necessity? Does one appreciate a nude painting, for instance, for purely aesthetic reasons? Likewise, whatever the value, intrinsic or otherwise, of trying to discover truth or create beauty, it seems that some measure of Aristotle's complaint about the externally dependent, sporadic, and mixed nature of such pleasures still appears to hold. Perhaps pure pleasure doesn't make for best leisure, but if it does, it's not clear to what extent A+ leisure constitutes an advance beyond the original view.

THE EDUCATIONAL SPLIT

Another part of the Aristotelean legacy, one that might take more effort to trace to its origin, is what we still think of today as not only a distinction but a dichotomy between two fundamentally different types of education. Philosopher John Dewey (1859–1952) traces this division back to ancient Greek culture in general but finds its exemplary expression in Aristotle: the fundamental split here is between the labour required for "merely living" and the leisure required for "living worthily" (268). Dewey attributes such a division, then as now, to a distinction between a largely uneducated but functionally necessary working class and a highly but not practically educated leisure class. Although slavery is no longer part of society, as it was in Aristotle's time, the cultural separation and presumed hierarchy between the two remains. It is, indeed, in the separate realms of education for two radically different forms of life that Dewey finds a fundamental roadblock to achieving true democracy.

"Probably the most deep-seated antithesis which has shown itself in education history," Dewey says, "is that between education in preparation for useful labour and education for a life of leisure" (266). In postsecondary terms we might think of the distinction between the curricula at a university and at a vocational school, respectively, or more messily yet more precisely, between the liberal arts and those courses of study, whether in university, community college, or trade schools, that purport to teach skills that are useful in a twofold sense: useful for the student's employment and society's deployment alike. As Dewey expresses the mindset of this Aristotelean legacy, "the less ... knowledge has to do with practical affairs, with making or producing, the more adequately it engages intelligence" (269). This is knowledge understood "as an end in itself, without reference to practice or even civic duties [that] is truly liberal or free" (270). This antithesis, if not entirely convincing, is certainly familiar.

Take, for example, the learning of languages. Although, in the Renaissance, much of what was worth reading was available only in Latin or Greek, and so the study of these languages had substantial intellectual value for accessing important literature, the cultural residue of this focus, though no longer so justified, remains. Betrand Russell puts it thus:

> It must be admitted that a great deal of the traditional cultural education was foolish. Boys spent many years acquiring Latin and Greek grammar, without being, at the end, either capable or desirous (except in a small percentage of cases) of reading a Greek or Latin author. Modern languages and history are preferable, from every point of view, to Latin or Greek. They are not only more useful, but they give much more culture in much less time. (21)

The traditional liberal arts, on this view, give the student not only a certain *breadth* of cultural exposure (and so are liberal in that sense), but also a *freedom* deriving from independent thought unhindered by practical concerns (and so are liberal in that sense as well).[1] The comparatively useless practice, at least for most contemporary students, of learning dead languages, was and to some extent remains a badge of the liberal breadth and freedom in the model of traditional education.

This kind of view inherits from Aristotle what we may call a "purity bias" exhibited in other parts of the culture as well. Just as Aristotle sees the best leisure as the purest, as valued intrinsically and not also instrumentally, we tend to think of cultural kinds as pure categories in terms of oversimplified, false dichotomies. Take sport, for example, which we tend to think of in terms of absolute contrasts with such other activities as games, martial arts, and dance, where any activity counts as belonging *at most* to one of these kinds and so not to any other. We may correctly identify chess as a game and dismiss it for that reason as a sport. But chess fails to be sport not because it is a game but because it is not the right type of game (i.e., it is not an *athletic* game). Similarly, some philosophers believe an activity can be a sport or an art but not both (Best 121), or a sport or a martial art but not both (Allen 249). Such views ignore the joint sport/art status of both figure skating and competitive dance (Holt, "Sport as Art" 145) and the joint sport/martial art status of taekwondo and judo, not to mention the practical application of combat sport techniques to self-defence scenarios (Holt, "Physical Philosophy" 3, 5). To sum up, then, the purity bias tends to yield questionable, oversimplified thinking about not only normative questions concerning the value of different leisure activities, but also descriptive questions concerning their classification.

If we try to bridge the gap between, in Dewey's terms, useful skill and liberal knowledge, either in culture generally or education specifically, not just any attempt will do. Indeed, for Dewey, "[i]t would be hard to find a subject

---

1 In his famous preface to *The Picture of Dorian Gray*, with perhaps merely apparent irony, Oscar Wilde states, "*All art is quite useless*" (8).

in the curriculum within which there are not found evil results of a compromise between the two opposed ideals" (274), with science praised for, but not taught with regard to, its practical application, and the arts praised for cultural importance but taught in the reductive mode of mastering professional techniques. This compromise, for Dewey, amounts to an "inorganic composite" that fails to resolve the educational split deriving from Aristotle (273).

So what is the solution? How do we achieve an organic synthesis in light of Dewey's concerns? It would seem that the solution is partly a matter of *regard* and partly a matter of *reform*, reform not only in education itself but in its principal focus as well. We need to acknowledge the intelligence, actual and potential, in the application of practical skills, and the potentiality of liberal arts to contribute, desirably and meaningfully, to being productive. More important, though, seems to be shifting focus to students themselves for, as Dewey puts it, "the development of a truly democratic society, a society in which all share in useful service and all enjoy a worthy leisure" (272). This means teaching students ostensibly on either side of the divide to appreciate and participate in the value of the other side.

Before moving on, we should note that when Dewey speaks of a worthwhile leisure, he falls in line with the Aristotelean tradition, augmented by Telfer, in which what really matters is the quality of leisure and other activities rather than the quantity. In light of this concern, we turn to a phenomenon where the quality of leisure becomes hollowed out in favour of a flagrant display of quantity and status.

CONSPICUOUS LEISURE

Picking up on the theme of the leisurely as marked by uselessness, we turn to Thorstein Veblen's (1857–1929) analysis of the leisure class, which takes uselessness not just as a sign but as a deliberate signal, a *badge*, a point of pride in the assertion of supposedly superior status.

In the Aristotelean worldview, again, the distinction between leisure and labour reflects not just differences between types of activity, but more fundamentally, as indicated in our discussion of Dewey above, between different social classes: the leisure class and the working class, respectively. Whether we consider historical distinctions between free citizens and slaves in the ancient world, or in medieval times between nobles and peasants, or in modern times between the wealthiest—the 1%—and the rest of us, the distinction is a familiar one. Since the advent of industrialization, of course, we also invariably speak of the middle class, usually distinguished in terms of having white collar as opposed to blue collar occupations, let alone the unemployed. The distinction between the "haves" and the "have nots" hardly needs mentioning. But where the ancient Greek ideal symbolizes a cultural apex, Veblen's analysis of the leisure class, both historically and in the modern era, outlines a way of living, a lifestyle, that is decidedly less productive and decidedly more decadent.

Considering leisure as exemplified by the leisure class, on Veblen's analysis, depends on a basic opposition between not only it and the working class but the opposed yet complementary values of the respective classes, with the importance of each acknowledged, at least implicitly, in the functioning and flourishing of society. The principal value of the working class, so defined, is productivity in providing for the essential needs and services of society. By contrast, indeed deliberate contrast, the principal value of the leisure class, whose needs have been provided for by the working class, is marked by and consists in the opposite, in *non*-productivity. Veblen puts it this way: "The characteristic feature of leisure class life is a conspicuous exemption from all useful employment" (31). It is not, however, simply that the leisure class enjoys in leisure the fruits of the labourers' labours. On Veblen's analysis it is not enjoyment of leisure that matters to the leisure class. What matters to them, rather, is that the resources and accoutrements of leisure are in his word *conspicuous*, where conspicuousness focuses outward from potential pleasure and instead on the *display* of such to others: "it is not sufficient merely to possess wealth or power. The wealth or power must be put in evidence, for esteem is awarded only by evidence" (29). Think of the role of social media in serving essentially the same purpose in today's society. Leisure becomes a medium for such self-assertion of status in seeking the esteem of others, whether they are seen as envious "lessers" or as more or less respected equals.

If this is the psychological and social dynamic at work within the leisure class, whatever its form, it should be clear that there are inherent problems with it, issues of morality and social justice that come to the fore. Despite the Aristotelean spirit of the social class distinction here, the image of the person of leisure so depicted is rather far removed from the image of the free citizen of ancient Athens. In modern iterations, the objective of the leisure class is to make one's station conspicuous, in a kind of "perpetual leisure," through no less conspicuous consumption. Think of the pointlessness of the billionaire's mega-yacht, or, on a lesser scale, the equally pointless self-assertive bragging of the stereotypical rap star. The more wasteful of resources, of time, money, goods, and services, and the more flagrantly displayed, the better. The absolute hollowness of such pointless, wasteful displays can hardly be exaggerated. What is chosen for leisure becomes reduced to instrumental motivation, playing for effect, rather than being in any real way intrinsically motivated. An enjoyment derived from impressing others is hollow indeed.

Veblen's analysis may be read as purely descriptive, as not meant to imply anything about the moral status of a leisure class that behaves as he describes. After all, one could accept this depiction of the leisure class without seeing anything wrong with that state of affairs, except perhaps the contingent complaint that one does not find oneself among the elite so depicted. One might instead read Veblen's analysis as saying less about how some privileged people choose to live and more about an unfortunate and unflattering tendency in human beings generally, that finding oneself among the leisure class might all but inevitably result in a perceived need to indulge such outward-focused, other-concerned displays of leisurely uselessness and consumption, with apparently no principled limit in the aspiration to display deliberately pointless and decadent lavishness. Despite being predicated on a similarly fraught distinction between social classes, the Veblen-style status-flaunter through wasteful leisure represents a complete reversal, a total inversion and hollowing out, of the Aristotelean leisure ideal, which is inner-focused, not outer-, self-concerned, not other-, and intellectually engaged and fulfilled, not disengaged and stunted.

REVIVING ARISTOTLE

Given problems identified by Dewey in the educational split and by Veblen in the analysis of the leisure class, it is no wonder that, for decades now, leisure theorists have, in one form or another, more or less explicitly, called for a revival of Aristotelean leisure, though without the attendant and inessential social injustices associated with that historical epoch and its cultural legacy. Whether this reclamation should include an expansion à la Telfer beyond intellectual contemplation as the purest form of leisure, what is clear is that many philosophers find in Aristotle's vision of leisure an antidote to the mere amusements of modern society, whether the pointedly wasteful displays of the leisure class, or the similarly shallow recreation of overworked or underemployed lower classes.

Consider, in conclusion, the following examples. De Grazia champions the Greek ideal of leisure as epitomized by Aristotle, for on that model "[t]he benefits of leisure are the benefits of cultivating the free mind" (394). Pieper likewise sees Aristotle, through the lens of his influence on Thomas Aquinas, as finding in leisure less the best of humanity and more our immanent divinity (51). Short of this, perhaps, Ramsay sees Aristotle as an "antidote to views of leisure as trivial, under-achieving, irrelevant to 'higher' activities [and as an] inspiration for leisure as an alternative to the social trivialization" of consumerism (13). The collective call to revive this part of Aristotle's legacy we should keep in mind as we continue on to the next chapter.

QUESTIONS FOR CONSIDERATION

- Do you think Telfer goes too far, or perhaps not far enough, in her account of A+ leisure?
- Is Telfer overly concerned with leisure being worthwhile? Does she conflate leisure with *good* leisure?
- Given the necessity of manual and domestic labour, why is it so often seen as "lesser" rather than essential?
- Are there some university programs that reflect the organic blend of intelligence and usefulness envisioned by Dewey?
- If leisure has become primarily a kind of *display*—think social media—can it ever be authentic?
- Is there any upside to leisure class leisure? Can it be productive?

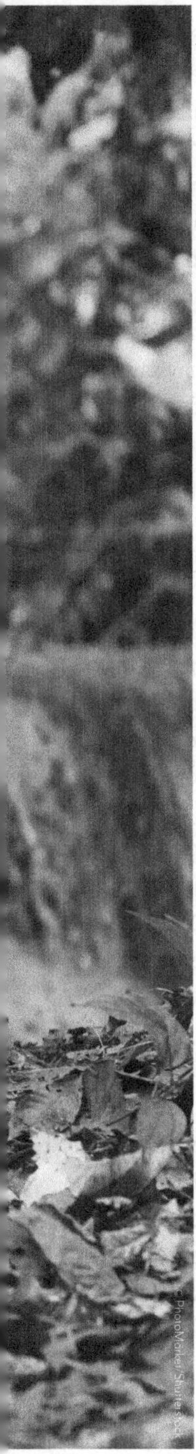

CHAPTER 4

Non-Western Views

We tend, somewhat uncritically, to think of leisure as a universal human phenomenon. But on reflection we might have legitimate concerns about the extent to which a concept of leisure arising in the Western tradition may apply only to that tradition. In this chapter we explore problems with and the potential for applying our concept of leisure to non-Western cultures, including Asian, African, and Indigenous North American. Although a Western understanding of leisure may not translate seamlessly into cross-cultural analysis, certain facets of non-Western cultures seem to exemplify a Western-derived concept of leisure or stand as reasonable analogues to some aspects of leisure in Western culture.

INTRODUCTION

In the previous two chapters we examined the beginning of significant philosophizing about leisure in the work of Aristotle, as well as the cultural legacy of that view from ancient times to the present day. Aside from more modern developments in the Western tradition's understanding of leisure, which we will consider in subsequent chapters, we now turn to analogous and alternative views that derive from other cultural traditions, Asian, African, and Indigenous North American cultures in particular. The point is not simply to observe that the Western tradition fails, for fairly obvious reasons, to give us the whole "story" of leisure, but to explore the scope and limits of what we may say about leisure in that tradition as potentially applying beyond itself to other cultures. We will probably fall short of a universal concept of leisure transparently readable into any culture whatsoever, but we may well find enough overlap and divergence with other cultures to suggest a broader, if not completely general, understanding of leisure based on but not circumscribed by, and extending appreciably beyond, Western culture itself.

First, however, a note on terminology is in order. By *Western* culture here I mean that culture or those cultures originating in Europe that spread to various parts of the world through colonialism, to the Americas and the Commonwealth of the former British Empire. We might call the tradition *Eurocentric* in this sense, but at the risk of marginalizing much Western theory developed beyond European borders that we will treat subsequently. Hence *Western* seems more appropriate in terms of connotation even though, geographically, Europe lies no further west than Africa, which for historical and cultural reasons tends to be set apart, in thought and in fact, from the culture we designate Western. My preference for *Western* over *Eurocentric*, then, is based on the lesser of possible confusions and a relative simplicity of expression.

CROSS-CULTURAL LEISURE

One apparent barrier to looking for leisure beyond the Western tradition is that many other cultures do not have a word for it. This is not universal, since there are some "terms in non-Western languages that appear to be consonant with, or at least similar to the English word 'leisure'," with some having derived from the English word (Yeh and Chick 2). The concern here is that cultures lacking a word for leisure may not have leisure at all. If they did have leisure they would also, presumably, have a word for it.

However, having some recognized cultural phenomenon doesn't require having a word for it in the language in question. For example, the German word *schadenfreude*, although lacking a corresponding word in English-speaking cultures, is perfectly understandable despite this lack (Yeh and Chick 3). But of course, *schadenfreude*—taking pleasure in others' suffering—has been anglicized. As it has become an English word, it is now obviously its own English-language equivalent.[1] Before anglicization, however, no doubt the phenomenon was intelligible to English speakers, as it is by those who happen to be unfamiliar with the word. The very fact that a word from one language and culture may be adopted into another seems to imply that cross-cultural analysis is limited less by vocabulary than by conceptual apparatus, although social phenomena such as leisure seem bound to vary cross-culturally, and so the problem will reemerge in another form.

Note first that German speakers and English speakers both belong to Western culture, and so the apparent ease of cross-cultural understanding here may not translate into non-Western contexts. For example, Fox mentions the case of the Hawaiian term *manawa nanea* (or "tranquil breath"), which seems like a rough synonym for leisure, although its detailed meaning is rendered as "lying in a shallow lagoon with water flowing over you while birds are singing" (404). Fox's point is that merely taking this phrase idiomatically as meaning simply leisure is likely to obscure layers of meaning (e.g., associations with not only enjoyment and relaxation, which are fitting, but with the heart and stomach, which seem elusive to the Western concept). This may be true, of course, but it seems linguistic investigation could expose any shortcomings in such attempts at translation. A literal example of reclining in flowing water with birdsong accompaniment might elicit a less than enthusiastic assent, in which case the expression might simply be an exemplar, again supporting an idiomatic interpretation. If nothing else, linguists and others bilingual in English and Hawaiian could straightforwardly identify how close the equivalence is, at what points it fails and by what margin. Other cultures aside, if we are unable, with some confidence, to identify leisure in native *Hawaiian* culture, something has gone wrong in our methods or assumptions.

Part of the answer seems to lie in activities common to both Asian and Western cultures that we readily identify as leisure in the latter. Take for example the reading and writing of poetry in Chinese culture (Wang and Stringer 38). This would probably strike us in most cases as a leisure activity. It may not be a leisure activity, of course, even in Western culture. If one writes poetry as an exercise in creative writing for university credit or on commission for a

1 *Kummerspeck* is a less familiar and thus better example. It literally means "grief bacon," i.e., weight gained from emotional overeating. The phenomenon may be familiar irrespective of knowing the word.

greeting card company, the activity will likely be extrinsically rather than intrinsically motivated, required rather than optional. Where these conditions do not apply, however, where the motivation is intrinsic and the activity elective, it could qualify as leisure in Asian as in Western culture.

Consider a useful example drawn from the philosophy of dance. Monroe Beardsley characterizes dance, in contrast to other movements and actions, in terms of unnecessary gestures, what he describes as a "superfluity of expressiveness" (35). He considers as a potential counterexample an Indigenous corn dance the choreography of which is a product of functional need rather than expressive choice. Even so, a performance of the pattern might strictly count as dance in Beardsley's sense:

> If *every* motion of the Corn Dance is prescribed in detail by magical formulas or religious rules to foster germination, growth, or a fruitful harvest, we might best regard it as pure ritual.... But if some part of what goes on in the ritual helps it to achieve expressiveness ... to some degree independent of any practical function.... If, in other words, there is more zest, vigor, fluency, expansiveness, or stateliness than appears necessary for its practical purposes, there is an overflow or superfluity of expressiveness to mark it as belonging to its own domain of dance. (35)

In other words, a performance of the pattern fails to count as dance if done, in all respects, for the sake of the harvest. If it is done for the sake of the harvest but leaves room for superfluous expression, it will count as dance, but not leisure. *If*, however, the pattern is performed unnecessarily, in celebration or in demonstration, say (Beardsley's example is competition), it may qualify not only as dance in Beardsley's sense (Holt, *Kinetic Beauty* 113), but also as leisure. In this way it seems cross-cultural analysis of leisure is not necessarily doomed to failure.

ASIAN LEISURE

We will now approach a cross-cultural analysis of leisure with respect to Western culture's most obvious contrast case: Asian, specifically East Asian, culture. It is a twofold approach. First, we will examine those philosophies that have prominently shaped many aspects of Asian culture, seeing whether and to what extent they allow for what Western eyes would recognize as leisure. Then we will look at Asian cultural analogues of leisure and related concepts to gauge how applicable our general understanding of leisure may be to cultures in which it did not originate. The upshot, perhaps, will be an understanding of leisure straddling the East-West divide and accommodating to some degree both perspectives.

Asian Philosophies

Three prominent philosophies come to the fore as significant influences on East Asian culture and thus as potential bases for understanding leisure in that culture: Confucianism, Buddhism, and Taoism (also written *Daoism*). We will briefly look at each in ascending order of plausibility to ground leisure that is recognizable to Western eyes.

Confucianism is the philosophy founded on the teachings of Confucius (K'ung Fu-Tzu) (551–479 BCE), in which emphasis is placed on doing one's duty and being motivated in so doing by one's feeling for humanity. The most important book in Confucianism is the *Analects*, and the moral ideal explored in that work and elsewhere is that of the *gentleman*. The gentleman is an educated and distinguished man characterized by right action in accordance with a doctrine of the mean not unlike Aristotle's, with right action walking a middle path between excess and deficiency. The gentleman cultivates himself, but not as in Western leisure, as an end in himself, but to be an effective leader: "He cultivates himself in order to bring peace to all people" (14.42). We might consider this peaceful tranquility to be a kind of leisure, but that would be misleading. It is more like accepting with equanimity one's lot in life, which for lower classes means doing *their* duty, which is largely arduous work. The one place for leisure in this outlook seems to be that the leaders themselves belong to a leisure class and so are able to cultivate themselves in a proper manner conducive to good leadership. The justification, however, even for such leisure is the appropriate functioning of society that depends on it. In Confucianism, then, we have something like an Aristotelean leisure class, but nothing really like Aristotelean leisure, except perhaps as may be enjoyed by a leader ruling best by simply occupying his proper place according to ritual. Confucius describes such a leader as one who "can be given a position facing south" (6.1).

Sticking with the theme of seated postures, we turn to Buddhism. Buddhism likely prompts the thought of meditation as its characteristic activity and as leisure par excellence. Indeed, the very icon of Buddhist philosophy is of countless representations of the Buddha seated in the lotus position, beaming with the contentment and tranquility of enlightenment, having achieved nirvana. This image is familiar and accessible enough to Western understanding. If nothing else, meditation seems to be an analogue to Aristotelean contemplation, but this impression is somewhat misleading. Meditation has an obvious and urgent purpose: to escape the suffering of life by freeing oneself from desire. It is a difficult process, "a kind of fiery baptism" (Suzuki 97). Nirvana is the reward promised for enduring this process, although from the outside meditation would seem worth doing for its own sake irrespective of such a lofty result. By contrast, Aristotelean contemplation is both process and product, activity and reward together. Even so, and as we will see in the next section, some forms of Buddhism suggest more nuanced parallels with Western understanding.

Probably the most leisure-friendly philosophy among major strands of Asian thought is Taoism. The foundational work of Taoism is the *Tao Te Ching* ("The Way and Its Power"), a book of verse, eighty-one verses in all, attributed to Lao Tzu (sixth century BCE). Where Confucianism stresses social engagement and doing one's duty, Taoism emphasizes instead withdrawal into solitude, tranquility, and living simply and modestly in harmony with nature (Lao Tzu 8). The exemplar here is not the Confucian gentleman or the Buddha himself but the sage. For Lao Tzu, the sage recognizes that our proper role is not to exert ourselves in action. Each of us is rather "to sit quietly and find the truth within" (5). It is not activity but "[s]tillness [that] reveals the truth of eternity" (16). This seems like Buddhist meditation as it appears from the outside, and to be a more plausible counterpart to Aristotelean contemplation than its Buddhist counterpart, though reason here is similarly deemphasized, a point we will return to below.

Taoism might seem impractical as a life-guiding philosophy, praising what we would regard as a life of a certain kind of leisure with work reduced to the bare minimum. However, this makes it a useful corrective to outlooks that overstress the importance of work. Perhaps paradoxically, it is also a source of excellent advice for getting things done. One example is Lao Tzu's anti-procrastination dictum, "Begin your task before it becomes a burden" (64). Such advice applies not only to the bare minimum of work required for simple subsistence but also to great tasks, as in the more famous line from the same verse, "A journey of a thousand miles begins with a single step" (64). Thus Taoism implies a quasi-leisurization of work in reducing tasks, either simple chores or great undertakings, to almost nothing, first doing only what is necessary, and second by seeing any task as no more than a small step that leads to a next step, then another, and another. This means avoiding the active struggle of effort and instead going with the flow, as we will see below.

Western Analogues

Considered on their own, as we saw above, Asian philosophical perspectives, each in different ways and to different degrees, leave significant room for leisure as understood in Western culture. We now turn to analogues in Eastern culture to leisure and cognate concepts as understood in the West, mostly from the Taoist tradition but also from the Buddhist, in particular Zen or Chan Buddhism.

First, the Taoist concept of *hsiao yao* (roughly "shao yow"), figuring prominently in the work of Chuang Tzu, is identified as a close analogue of the classical Western concept of leisure as a "cultivation of self" and "freedom from the necessity of being occupied" (Yeh and Chick 1). *Hsiao yao* liberates one from constraints, both outward demands and inner turmoil and rigid thinking, to experience instead a harmonious, tranquil way of being. "For Chuang Tzu, *hsiao yao* implied freedom, happiness, a liberation of mind, the effortless state of being, and the ultimate state of being" (Yeh and Chick 8). The influence of *hsiao yao* on Asian perspectives on leisure is profound. "In fact, this philosophy can be viewed not only as a leading Chinese philosophy of leisure but also as having [a] profound impact on the formation of later Chinese ideas of leisure" (Yeh and Chick 9). What makes *hsiao yao* possible is a state of being called *wu-wei* ("woo way"), meaning "no-action," which is "a natural course of action not driven by any motive of gain or striving" (Yeh and Chick 9), where one lets things happen naturally, including one's own actions, rather than trying to force them.

The "no-action" of *wu-wei* ties in with a similar notion of "no-mind" in the Buddhist tradition, in particular Zen or Chan Buddhism.[2] The idea of "no-mind"—*mushin* ("moo shin") in the Japanese, *wuxin* ("woo shin") in the Chinese—is a state of mind and body where one is not mindless or unconscious but rather focused appropriately and not distracted by irrelevant thoughts or environmental stimuli, either of which could remove one from the task at hand and one's ability to respond fluidly and quickly to the dynamic of one's situation. This state of mind and body is championed in many Asian martial arts (Holt, "Physical Philosophy" 4–5), and may be seen as the more active counterpart to the passive, effortless—though by no means inactive—state of *wu-wei*. In this way, Zen "no-mind" bears a striking similarity to the Western notion of being in a flow state (Krein and Ilundáin 160), where one is "in the zone," performing well and almost effortlessly, which is itself the more active counterpart to the standard, comparatively passive type of

2 *Zen* designates the Japanese and *Chan* the Chinese versions of this type of Buddhism.

aesthetic experience (Holt, *Kinetic Beauty* 33). Thus between "no-action" and "no-mind" it seems we run the gamut of Asian leisure from its most passive to its most active forms.

Relatedly, the Taoist ideal of inner peace through living in accordance with nature bears striking affinities to certain views in the Western tradition, Epicureanism and especially Stoicism, the ideal of which is often expressed in virtually the same terms (Seneca 216–17). In both worldviews the human being is a microcosm of the world at large, and living rightly, living well, means aligning oneself with the universe of which one is a part. For Taoists it is the *Tao* (Way) that governs the universe, whereas for the Stoics it is the *Logos* (Reason). The following comment on Chuang Tzu, second in distinction among Taoists only to Lao Tzu, could have come from any Greek or Roman Stoic: "If one properly understands the natural order of things, of which death is a part, then fear and mourning will no longer be necessary" (Osborne and van Loon 135). But the analogy is imperfect. First, *wu-wei* as going with the flow seems to suggest a more pleasure-based Epicurean than reason-based Stoic outlook. More importantly, where the Stoics see the universe as fundamentally *rational*, Taoists see it rather as fundamentally *organic*. As Osborne and van Loon put it, "Taoists aimed at a life of simplicity, not being ruled by intellect, but by a natural power, or Te" (129). For Taoists, nature makes sense, but it is not rational. For Stoics, it is supremely rational.

Where the analogy with Stoicism fails, however, we find yet another parallel with the West, but in popular rather than high culture: the fictional universe of *Star Wars*. The fictional *Star Wars* universe is governed by "the Force," a blend of Tao and Te, the Way and its Power, tapped into by the good Jedi and the evil Sith. As Obi-Wan Kenobi describes it in the original film, "The Force is what gives a Jedi his power. It's an energy field created by all living things. It surrounds us and penetrates us and binds the galaxy together" (qtd. in Wetmore 94). As we see him in *The Empire Strikes Back* and *Return of the Jedi*, the character of Yoda, Jedi mentor to Obi-Wan Kenobi and Luke Skywalker, lives a secluded simple life on Dagobah, a swamp planet teeming with life, in many ways the epitome of the Taoist sage (Wetmore 95). In the prequel trilogy we see Yoda in a much more Confucian mode, serving the Republic as head of the Jedi Council before going into Taoist exile. The sci-fi context aside, the metaphysics of the *Star Wars* universe is essentially Asian and mostly Taoist. If nothing else, such popularization of Taoist thought for Western audiences helps us understand the leisure potential of its original Asian form.

RESISTING COLONIAL LEISURE

Turning from fictional to actual empires, we will now look at African and Indigenous leisure through the lens of clashes with colonial cultures. Relevant to this discussion will be how colonial cultures interpret and impose themselves on native cultures, and how those cultures interpret themselves and respond to colonial oppression.

In the confrontation between African and colonial cultures we find a tendency of the latter to reductively gloss and underappreciate traditional native leisure and to prescribe alternatives deemed more appropriate. According to Naidoo, for example, traditional leisure in Nigeria includes "activities such as festivals, moonlight stories, meetings at the village square, hunting, dancing, wrestling, fishing, swimming, and playing various types of games during free time" (93). Colonial cultures tended to view such traditional leisure as either "wasting time" or mere "celebrations of life" (Naidoo 94), thus failing to appreciate the layers of social and spiritual significance of such practices that depart from Western culture's emphasis on time-management and individual freedom. This failure of colonial understanding neglects a significant parallel with the Western tradition as expressed by Pieper, according to whom, for instance, "[t]he festival is the origin of leisure, and the inward and ever-present meaning of leisure" (49). The corresponding tendency, then, is to introduce leisure activities that are "more appropriate," such as the European game of soccer, that for Africans themselves, initially, were neither intrinsically motivated nor truly elective. The irony here is that under colonial rule and in the post-colonial era, African cultures came to accept and truly leisurize European imports like soccer, seeing them as platforms for individual expression and national pride (Naidoo 95–96). Along with efforts to preserve traditional forms of leisure, we find certain aspects of colonial leisure appropriated by evolving African cultures.

Similar phenomena are in evidence when we consider conflicts between settler colonialism and Indigenous cultures. Here, too, we find leisure activities such as sports to be sites of colonial oppression and Indigenous resistance to such oppression (Forsyth et al. 18). In terms in Indigenous North American culture, for instance, the subculture of an introduced settler sport such as ice hockey may reinforce both racial stereotypes and the dominance of settler colonialism, while yet providing opportunities for leisure success and personal transformation through self-expression and achievement in the face of oppression. Traditional Indigenous sports and games such as lacrosse may have succumbed partly to settler cultural appropriation, reducing them to "mere pastimes" without regard for their social or spiritual significance

(Rice 30–32). However, keeping alive an Indigenous understanding of lacrosse as something shared with the gods, as a healthy substitute for war, and as honoring ancestors (Rice 34), reveals such activities to be not just leisure in a robust sense but something much greater.

Part of our ability to engage in such cross-cultural understanding of leisure seems to depend on recognizing that we are often dealing with something *more* than leisure in terms of cultural significance and *less* than leisure in terms of individual self-concern. Part of the story is that different cultural values are at work where the community overshadows what, from a Western perspective, may be seen as the pivotal importance of the individual (though Taoism is an exception here, and to some extent Buddhism as well). In some African cultures, for instance, the principle of *ubuntu* is operative, a "communal ethics that maintains that a person is a person through other people" (Meynell and Paron 138). A comparable communal ethics can be seen in many Indigenous cultures in North America, where an individual often sees themselves in terms of "all my relations," including not just family and fellow tribespeople but also ancestors, future generations, gods, animals, plants, and even non-living things (Meynell and Paron 68). As we will see below, such differences constitute a real but not necessarily insurmountable challenge in doing cross-cultural analysis of leisure.

"THE WAY OF OUR PEOPLE"

We have seen how non-Western cultures have at least analogues of leisure and possibly just different cultural expressions of the need for leisure generally. Except for Taoist and, to a lesser extent, Buddhist perspectives, however, the Western emphasis on individual choice in leisure appears not to fit well with Asian, African, and Indigenous perspectives emphasizing instead relations to social groups. The apparent discontinuity may be partly overcome by Western views emphasizing leisure as a type of divine worship through social festivities. Likewise, the prioritizing of social groups does not obviously preclude personal choice and expression in leisure contexts, however socially circumscribed. Indeed, the *elective* character of leisure activities may fall partly to the individual and partly to the community. So long as intrinsically motivated activities are the product of genuine choice—say, community rather than personal choice—we respect the definition of leisure as intrinsically motivated elective activities applying in non-Western cultures as well. This application depends on drawing a meaningful distinction in non-Western contexts between nature and culture, either from within or outside such cultural contexts. In a culture that sees itself inextricably entwined with the natural world, this separation may not be possible from within the culture itself.

We might find that such a culture fails to distinguish cultural choice from natural necessity, if, for instance, both are subsumed under the general concept of "the way of our people." This conflation, however, poses no special barrier to using our perspective to explain leisure and cognate phenomena in other cultures—unless, that is, the cultural aspects of such communities are seen as no less "necessary," no less "natural," than the requirements of biological subsistence. Where a culture's tradition is held to be entirely self-justifying, we may correctly identify a specific naturalistic fallacy lurking here: the appeal to tradition. That is, a cultural practice may be an expression of community freedom even if members of that community uncritically regard it as necessary rather than chosen. Even here, however, the necessity will be conditional rather than categorical, because cultures will require various commitments from their members, ethical and otherwise, but invariably acknowledge the possibility and reality of different ways of being, even if the culture in question regards itself as superior.

The plausibility of cross-cultural leisure analysis depends minimally on being able to distinguish, more or less objectively, between what it means to live and what it means to live a certain way. We can hypothesize with some claim to objectivity what constitutes necessity and what amounts to individual or collective choice, and what motivates the latter, in cultures other than our own. This will suffice to make justified if tentative claims about cross-cultural leisure.

QUESTIONS FOR CONSIDERATION

- Which of the major Eastern philosophies—Confucianism, Buddhism, and Taoism—do you find most appealing, and to what extent does your choice reflect your own attitudes about leisure?
- Do you see other parallels between Asian and Western leisure besides those discussed above?
- How should Westerners approach dialogue about leisure with non-Western cultures that have historically suffered under colonialism?
- Can sharing in leisure from other cultures help build cross-cultural understanding? If so, how? What are the risks involved?
- How important is it to preserve more traditional forms of leisure in the face of new possibilities introduced by other cultures? Does it depend on which culture we are talking about?
- To what extent are leisure activities *prescribed* by a culture able to preserve leisure status?

CHAPTER 5

Time for Reflection

In this chapter we examine different concepts of time and how they affect the way we think about and practice leisure. We begin with how the modern concept of time, despite its advantages, threatens to undermine leisure possibilities in contemporary society. Time has become commodified, a quantity the quality of which is marginalized or ignored. As a corrective, we can look to more qualitatively informed concepts of time and leisure, not just to non-Western perspectives but earlier eras in our own culture, and also look through a qualitative, reflective lens at leisure possibilities available to us, and that we may work toward, even in a consumerist culture that makes doing so more difficult.

INTRODUCTION

We tend to think of opportunities for leisure in broader terms like *time off*, in contrast to being at work or on the clock. A long weekend is better, all else being equal, because it is *more* time off. This common if impoverished sense of leisure as discretionary time, or leisure time, certainly captures that part of our definition of leisure allowing for elective activities, and we tend to think of such activities as intrinsically motivated. As we have seen, however, there is such a thing as elective work, which is not required but chosen, and some off-work activities may be chosen for purely instrumental reasons. Thus a temporal understanding of leisure tends to make us think quantitatively rather than qualitatively about having if not fulfilling the leisure to choose the activities we wish. In modern times, this mindset has resulted in the commodification of time and of leisure.

Exploring this problem will occupy us throughout this chapter, and addressing it will depend on critical analysis of the status quo in thinking about leisure time and alternative perspectives on time and leisure promoting a more qualitative and reflective mindset. Such alternatives include premodern views of time and leisure in the Western tradition and similar insights from non-Western cultures. In leisure we have an opportunity for deep and meaningful reflection, one that, to our detriment, we often neglect.

CONCEPTS OF TIME

Just as we tend to think of leisure in terms of time off, we likewise tend to think of time itself in simple, straightforward ways. Time is something that passes, that moves events from future to present to past. Events happen *in* time and processes take place *over* time. Time is also something we use. We use it to measure duration, in hours, minutes, seconds, in days, weeks, months. We use clocks to time things, and we set clocks according to conventions to coordinate with other people and society at large, to control time spent at work or at play, and to be able to begin and end such activities precisely as we often wish. Our concept of time allows us to use it, not just precisely but in some respects very well.

This commonsense understanding of time seems obvious and inevitable. What other senses of time could there be? We might note, first, that this common sense of time is different in some respects from time as understood in a technical sense by physicists and philosophers. Such theoretical concepts of time put it, for instance, on par with the three dimensions of space: not things in space *and* time but things in spacetime. Likewise, if we imagine a God's-eye perspective allowing one to "see" all events—past, present, and future—at once, time and change appear to be unreal, a necessary illusion for beings like us. More to the point, however, a modern Western understanding of time differs significantly from ancient and medieval understandings in the Western tradition and Eastern traditions alike. The concept of time, in other words, is malleable, and different concepts of time have different implications for how we perceive leisure and how we pursue leisure.

At the risk of oversimplification, we can distinguish between and usefully juxtapose ancient and modern concepts of time. The former was more prominent in earlier eras, is more leisure-friendly, and is also typical of non-Western cultures. The latter is more prominent in contemporary culture, obviously, is in many ways less leisure-friendly, and has mostly displaced ancient conceptions of time in non-Western cultures as well.

Following Goodale and Godbey (128–29), we can draw the distinction along the following lines. The ancient concept of time is psychological and subjective, whereas the modern concept is clock-based and objective. Ancient time is tied to the natural world, modern time to the mechanized world. Ancient time, as tied to nature, is cyclical—think of a circle—a matter of day changing to night and night to day, of one season leading to the next in a regular, repeating pattern. Detached from nature, modern time is linear—think of an arrow—extending uniformly into the past and future alike. Ancient time is something that passes irrespective of us, whereas modern time is something we think of as a thing we can control. Ancient time is endless, eternal, whereas modern time is finite, definite. Ancient time is unmeasured but for "units" suggested by nature itself, days, years, and so on, whereas modern time is not only measured precisely but standardized to coordinate activities in different locales and across the world.

Ancient	Modern
Psychological	Clock-based
Natural	Mechanized
Cyclical	Linear
Passing	Controlled
Endless	Finite
Unmeasured	Standardized

TABLE 5.1 *Concepts of time*

This juxtaposition of ancient and modern concepts of time may seem loaded, as if modern time were simply wrongheaded or pointless. Admitting its problematic implications for leisure, though, the modern concept of time is a mixed but indispensable blessing. The modern concept of time and all its associated technological and theoretical benefits could not be dispensed with without seriously undermining much of the social and intellectual progress without which we can't even characterize, much less distinguish, modern Western society from premodern and non-Western cultural landscapes. The modern concept is to our credit as well as to our detriment.

Before assessing in more detail the negative effects on leisure of the modern concept of time, we should bear in mind that even if a complete return to ancient time is undesirable and unfeasible, we can mindfully make significant room for it in our lives. Later we will look at accounts of how this might play out. For now, we can acknowledge that even if we superficially divide modern time between that spent in work and other prescribed ways and that spent otherwise, whatever free time we do have, qualitative reflection on how we spend it and how we ought to is nonetheless possible. Whether this is a matter of returning to older, more spiritual ways of celebrating and affirming life, or mindfully reflecting on what would constitute meaningful, fulfilling leisure on a personal level in contemporary society, we will turn to explore subsequently.

TIME AS COMMODITY

Modern clock time is terribly useful of course, in myriad ways. Think about how much of your typical day is bound up, either explicitly or implicitly, with standardized time and the ability to track it precisely. But the predominant tendency is not to use clocks in service of human purposes, though that certainly does happen, but rather to use *ourselves* for the sake of clock-defined purposes, to make the *best* use of our time, not for the sake of leisure but rather for the sake of productivity. We don't use clocks so much as clocks use us, a phenomenon sometimes referred to as the "tyranny of the clock" (Goodale and Godbey 129). This state of affairs might be difficult to discern if we have been living under such an assumption most of our lives without questioning it. To the extent that our lives feel not just busy but pressured, hectic, and harried, the notion that we suffer under the tyranny of the clock becomes more plausible, and even obvious. Not everyone feels this way, of course, or to the same degree, or ought to for that matter, but that in no way invalidates the view.

One important part of this phenomenon is what we can think of as the modernization paradox: that although modern society has a much higher *potential* for leisure for most people than in times past, there appears to be much less *actual* leisure in modern times compared with earlier eras (Goodale and Godbey 130–31). Many of us have a forty-hour work week, which we think of as a lot. Indeed, there are various efforts to institute a four-hour workday or four-day work week. In times past, however, nothing prevented employers from cruelly overworking employees till they dropped. (This is not to say that the problems of worker exploitation do not persist, since clearly they do.) Forty hours a week of many kinds of work leave a lot of people a lot of time and sufficient energy for leisure. Time for leisure is there, but that time often seems to be ill-used from a leisure-forward perspective if we devote that time to doing extra work, chores, keeping in shape, and so on. We still choose such activities on some level, and yet a modern concept of time and an efficiency-motivated work ethic threaten to "workify" leisure itself.

Explaining this modernization paradox involves appealing to people's motives and perceptions of social values and duties, all framed at least implicitly by a modern concept of time. As far as motive is concerned, people are, naturally enough, disposed to want *more*, that is, more specifically, more of the good or what is believed to be good. But even if the good that people should want more of is leisure or found in leisure, the contemplative leisure of an Aristotelean or a Taoist, say, under a modern concept of time, together with certain unreflective ideas of value, it is *not* leisure that many people want more of, but rather money and social status (Goodale and Godbey 131). These are goods, of course, but their value is instrumental rather than intrinsic. They are good because of what they can be used to do, not in themselves. Money can be used to buy things that are either essential, like food, or elective, like leisure experiences. Money has no value in itself, although it is often so regarded, as if the point of being rich is just to be rich, or to satisfy arbitrary desires, and not to be able to do good.

Wanting more money or status, even if one has plenty, induces people to choose overwork for the sake of accumulating more of the good; this means often neglecting opportunities for envisioning, reflecting on, and enjoying good ends, like leisure in a robust sense. In such a culture, the primary "social value" is presumed to be *production*, and the primary "social duty" *consumption* (Goodale and Godbey 131–32). In a rather reductive sense of this viewpoint, we choose to work hard for the economy and, as it were, our purchase on it, rather than the economy working for us. Where we do not have to, we may work for greater economic power or status rather than truly for ourselves and our own enjoyment, that is, for our leisure.[1] This accords with

---

1 This suggests another paradox that Linder refers to in the title of his book, *The Harried Leisure Class*.

Veblen's account, as we saw earlier, of the leisure class indulging in conspicuous consumption to affirm and flaunt an elevated social status. Where the truly wealthy do not have to work for such disposable resources, many of the rest of us choose to do so.

To clarify just how it is that time has been commodified, consider what is sometimes referred to as the temporal cost argument. As Goodale and Godbey express this argument, paraphrasing de Grazia, "[w]hat we want today are things, things cost money, money costs time" (131). This enthymeme implies a transitive relationship between things and time through money,[2] from which it follows that things cost time, and what we want today is time. By *goods* here we might include not only material goods but also services and, more abstractly, experiences, which are often purchasable and in that sense commodified, along with the time we trade in work for money to spend on necessary and leisure activities alike. Thus the commodification of time as something to buy, as a qualitatively undifferentiated quantity, threatens to imply a commodification of leisure itself as reduced to qualitatively undifferentiated quantities that may be purchased as leisure experiences. Thus it becomes the *amount* of leisure available that seems to matter, not the *kind* of leisure available. Our leisure preferences will be expressed within comparatively narrow spheres of purchasable selections.

The implications of commodified time, for Goodale and Godbey, include seeing ourselves and our leisure pursuits as limited by and bound up with commerce, with what we can devote time to for the sake of spending money on whatever, giving rise to new dilemmas (136–38). Goods have become more plentiful but less useful. We have become more attached to things in general than things that are special or unique. We are into fungibility, interchangeability, rather than rarity or uniqueness. There is a greater pressure to take and make time as a *scarce* commodity, since it invariably seems less in supply than we would want. Even in terms of free time, there is a tension between the objective fact of having more of it than we used to and the subjective feel of having less. The solution to many of these dilemmas doesn't appear to be either paternalistic interference in other people's lives or securing even more free time for them to do with as they will, but rather a wholesale shift in people's attitudes, which will occupy us for the rest of the chapter.

2 Transitivity means that if A implies B, and B implies C, it follows that A implies C.

CELEBRATING LIFE

One antidote to the modern concept of time, or its negative side at any rate, may be found in the highly influential book by Josef Pieper, *Leisure the Basis of Culture* (1948), a seemingly paradoxical title, since leisure, true leisure, is supposed to be valuable in itself rather than as a basis for something else valuable, in this case culture. Here we should remember the contrast between nature and culture, with natural necessity (e.g., shelter) contrasted with variable and partly arbitrary expressions in meeting essential needs (e.g., architecture) and non-essential activities aside from such necessities (e.g., playing games indoors). We can dispel the appearance of paradox in Pieper's title by considering culture not as something separate from leisure but as consisting in leisure itself. Thus culture finds its basis in leisure because, in a very real sense, culture *is* leisure. What this means for Pieper we will now explore in some detail.

We can see the modern concept of time reflected in Pieper's characterization of *the worker* as a type. The worker embodies not only a work ethic in which value is grounded in efforts at production, but also an efficiency ethic in which one's efforts are put to best use in maximizing productivity. As idealized, the worker exhibits three characteristics identified by Pieper: "extreme tension in the powers of action" rather than a playful or carefree comportment; "readiness to suffer *in vacuo* [i.e., in isolation] unrelated to anything," as if extreme effort to the point of suffering were valuable in itself irrespective of function or objective; and "complete absorption in the social organism" rather than prioritizing one's experiences or oneself, society being "rationally planned to utilitarian ends," where the common good takes priority irrespective of individual preferences or pleasures (43). From such a perspective, even the best leisure appears nothing but "laziness, idleness, and sloth" (43), rather than the ultimate purpose for which we work at all.

In this regard, where leisure is the antithesis of work, Pieper points to *acedia* ("uh-*see*-dee-uh") as the corresponding vice, being disposed to a kind of depressed or restless "idleness" (44, 46). This is not, for Pieper, the vice of sloth, of not being disposed to work at all, but a kind of off-work failure of contentment that betrays an incapacity for leisure, a need, a compulsion, to stay busy. The insidious vice, for Pieper, is not a lack of practical wherewithal or a failure to pull one's own weight, though these are certainly issues worth confronting, but in the end a rejection of human dignity and one's share in it, a failure to accept, much less affirm or celebrate, existence as it is. It is a rejection of oneself as a worthy being, and of one's place in the world. In such a mindset, what one has, what one *is*, is never enough.

Contrasting with both work and acedia, real leisure, according to Pieper's view, is calm rather than restless, not just or necessarily a matter of outward calm, but more importantly, "an attitude of inward calm, or silence," and "not being busy, but letting things happen" (46). It is "the direct opposite of effort" and "opposed to the exclusive idea of work *qua* social function" (49). Pieper's view of leisure draws on Aristotle but adds the important element of saying *yes* to life, a "contemplative 'celebration'" of life and an affirmation of existence (48–49). We find such leisure both grounded and peaking in social festivals: "[t]he festival is the origin of leisure, and the inward and ever-present meaning of leisure" (49). Pieper's picture of leisure is of a heavily psychological and essentially spiritual state of being that is both essentially human yet also transcendent.

At the heart of Pieper's view is that leisure is essentially a spiritual state of being, specifically a kind of religious attitude. As he puts it, "leisure can only be made possible and justifiable on the same basis as the celebration of a festival. *That basis is divine worship*" (65). Bringing up divine worship here may seem to come out of nowhere, since of course there are plenty of pagan and secular festivals that would not count as divine worship. But Pieper is working with an often if not always implicitly Christian and specifically Catholic understanding of divine worship. Indeed, though he does not say so explicitly, he might hold up his Catholic view of leisure to be the antithesis of the Protestant work ethic the more compulsive and excessive aspects of which he targets directly.

We do not need to wade into stubborn debates between diverse traditions of Christian thought here. Suffice it to say, Pieper seems to allow for various other aspects of leisure besides, and presumably independent of, its alleged basis, different forms of divine worship or spirituality, along with potentially secular activities. "The celebration of divine worship ... is the deepest of the springs by which leisure is fed and continues to be vital—though it must be remembered that leisure embraces everything which, without being *merely* useful, is an essential part of a full human existence" (69–70). This would include not only parts of Western leisure outside the sphere of divine worship, some spiritual and some secular, but also leisure in non-Western cultures. Think of community-based festivals no less fulfilling of leisure's promise in Asian, African, and Indigenous cultures, informed by the principles of respectively Confucian, *ubuntu*, and relational worldviews. As for leisure on an individual scale in contemporary culture, this will become more of a focal point next.

REFLECTIVE LEISURE

Hayden Ramsay offers an account of leisure, specifically what he calls reflective leisure, very much in the spirit of Pieper's. As Pieper opposes leisure to acedia and an overemphasized work ethic, Ramsay sets up reflective leisure as the corrective to unreflective leisure choices in consumerist society. Pieper's worker and Ramsay's consumer are two sides of the same coin, effectively variations on a single theme.

One difference in Ramsay's approach is to admit, not that leisure has been lost and needs to be reclaimed, but that the meaning of leisure itself has changed for the worse, and we simply can't go back (31). Ours is a consumerist society, one largely understood in terms of the production and consumption of goods and services. In pre-consumerist societies—think ancient, medieval, and early modern cultures—leisure activities depended on minimal economic resources. But in such consumerist societies as ours, by contrast, leisure activities tend to be resource-based and understood primarily if not exclusively as such. Where a medieval peasant might take a day off to fish in the local river, a fishing vacation nowadays will often involve significant time and expense for travel, equipment, guides, and other resources.

On the plus side, such leisure experiences are "democratic," available to all who have sufficient resources, yet not everyone has such resources. Furthermore, leisure itself, as we saw earlier with time, has become *commodified* in consumerist culture (31). Ramsay diagnoses the problem not necessarily in consumerism itself, although he does frame consumerism as inherently problematic, but in the fact that we often fail to reflect mindfully on the choices we make and the kinds of choices available to us (32). For Ramsay, the alternative to such unreflective consumerist leisure is *reflective* leisure, not a going back to pre-consumerist leisure, since that is both impossible and to some extent undesirable, but evolving into a culture characterized by post-consumerist leisure.

On its face, consumerism appears to offer a narrow set of values among others, which we may buy into at certain times, and to certain degrees, but opt out of at others. In Ramsay's view, however, it is rather more insidious, offering a "total logic," providing serious answers to questions of what to value and what to do, systematically informing our evaluation of things and possibilities, and—crucially here—excluding other views (37). Part of the problem with consumerist leisure is the overwhelming tendency toward hedonistic, mindless activities, easily commodified, often addictive, and seldom edifying leisure experiences. Consumerist leisure, as Ramsay sees it, is twofaced, as "[t]he nice face expresses increased freedom and individual choice" (37). But this nice face comes at a cost that is not just literal, since "the nasty face of consumerist leisure expresses acquisitiveness, possessiveness, ... the desire for more than one's appropriate share" (38). This is in part because consumerist leisure tends to offer a genuine range of ultimately superficial, empty choices in contrast to the more meaningful, fulfilling choices of reflective leisure, to which we now turn.

What makes for reflective leisure in Ramsay's sense is twofold: activities which are not mindless but mindful, where one is able to reflect not just *in* the activities themselves but *on* the activities themselves as worthy leisure choices. As Ramsay puts it, reflective leisure "combines freedom from pressures, activity for its own sake, and reflection on meaning ..." (49), including elements of both Aristotelean contemplation and Pieperian appreciation. Such activities include the following categories: (1) intellectual, such as reading; (2) spiritual, such as meditating; (3) relational, such as getting together with friends; (4) aesthetic, such as doing arts and crafts; and (5) physical, such as playing sports. These, of course, are not mutually exclusive categories. If one participates in a marital art such as taekwondo, for instance, one can identify elements running the gamut, from obvious physical and social benefits to opportunities for creative self-expression, moving meditation, and embodied philosophy (Holt, "Physical Philosophy" 4–5). You might consider, as an exercise, to which of the five categories above your favourite leisure activities belong.

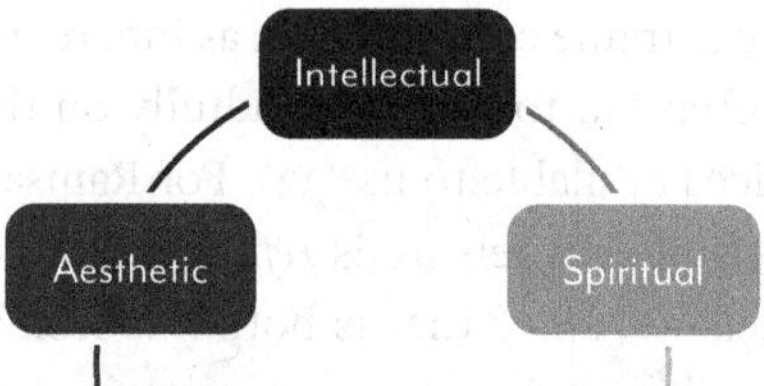

FIGURE 5.1 *Types of reflective leisure*

To be clear, an activity often done for the sake of leisure is no guarantee of its status as leisure, much less reflective leisure. One can read mindlessly as well as mindfully, for instance, or out of a sense of duty rather than choice. If one feels obligated to relax or to participate in certain forms of recreation that one judges to be worthwhile, that jeopardizes the leisure status of those activities. Ramsay is aware of this pitfall, and enjoins us to preserve leisure in a reflective vein by focusing on play (56). He acknowledges that play and reflection seem incompatible. Play is physical and emotional where reflection is intellectual, juvenile rather than mature, easy rather than difficult, and natural rather than cultural (Ramsay 52). It is not that these distinctions can't be drawn—they can—but rather that they do not constitute a dichotomy.

Indeed, it is precisely in leisure that reflective meaning and joyful play may come together (53). If play is at the heart of true leisure, then it behooves us to turn our attention next to the nature of play itself.

QUESTIONS FOR CONSIDERATION

- To what extent can and should we make room in our lives for an ancient concept of time, and what would that involve?
- Do some people escape the "tyranny of the clock"? Is that always a good thing, and if not why not?
- To what extent do Pieper's and Ramsay's accounts complement each other in the diagnosis of and prescription for problems in modern leisure?
- Is affirming our existence through festivals necessarily spiritual, and if so, in what sense? Could spirituality be broader than Pieper's view seems to suggest?
- Are there facets of consumerist leisure that Ramsay undervalues, and if so, how does that affect his view?
- Does emphasizing the importance of reflective leisure go too far and undermine certain aspects or forms of unreflective leisure?

CHAPTER 6

Being at Play

This chapter examines play as an important cognate concept of leisure helping enrich our understanding of leisure itself. In particular, we will discuss two theories of play that have achieved some prominence in the philosophy of leisure literature. The first is Huizinga's theory of the nature and cultural significance of play, the latter infused in not just leisure contexts but also more widely in the culture at large. The second of these is Nash's theory of play as especially suited to the innate human propensity toward being active, whether in leisure or work contexts. Nash also proposes a qualitative hierarchy among different types of play-based leisure activities in which the roles of activity and creativity are paramount.

INTRODUCTION

Examining play as a close cousin of leisure will help us triangulate the latter. Recall that leisure is defined as intrinsically motivated elective activities, and play is not only similar to, but in some ways seems to lie at the heart of, leisure itself. Activities are playful when those performing them are doing so for the sake of fun and enjoyment. Thus play often provides the intrinsic motivation for leisure activities. In another sense, certain types of activities that are typically chosen rather than necessary are often referred to as activities we play. Although play fails to overlap with all forms or uses of leisure, and includes examples outside the scope of leisure as well, it nonetheless illuminates certain aspects of leisure itself.

Although the two theories of play to be discussed in this chapter differ in approach and focus, they share a commitment to the vital importance of play in understanding human psychology and culture, in what it means to be human at all. Johan Huizinga offers a social theory of play as something both different from ordinary life and yet suffusing all aspects of human culture. Jay B. Nash (1886–1965), on the other hand, offers a psychological theory of play stressing activity and creativity and suggests a qualitative hierarchy among different types of leisure activities as ways of fulfilling the natural human impetus toward playful activity.

HUIZINGA ON PLAY

The premise of Huizinga's theory of play is strikingly similar to Pieper's theory of leisure. Specifically, just as Pieper positions leisure at the very foundation of human culture, Huizinga assigns such a foundational role not to leisure per se but rather to play. The title of Pieper's book, *Leisure the Basis of Culture*, and the subtitle of Huizinga's book *Homo Ludens* ("playing man"), *A Study of the Play-Element in Culture*, suggest a provocative if unintentional kinship. Where Pieper sees human culture as distinguished by its leisure, Huizinga sees it as distinguished by its play, even in decidedly non-leisurely cultural domains.

The Nature of Play

Huizinga provides an analysis of play in terms of various basic features. Before broaching that, however, it will be helpful to distinguish three different senses of the term "play" figuring in different ways, often implicitly, in Huizinga's account. Much of what Huizinga says about play can seem curious in comparison with what he says about play elsewhere unless one bears in mind that he has different senses of the term in mind. To take an example, Huizinga pictures play as distinct from everyday life but also as permeating the entire culture, including everyday life! Being charitable to Huizinga's account will require us to keep different senses of play in mind as we go, to appreciate how different aspects of this complex phenomenon can come to the fore and recede in different cultural contexts.

The three senses of play to distinguish, and to keep in mind as we proceed, I will refer to as the attitude sense, the activity sense, and the acting sense, respectively, where play depends, respectively, on a person's mindset, the type of activity participated in, or a certain kind of pretense, a special blend of the other two senses of play. We will discuss each of these senses in turn.

In the attitude sense, what will count as play depends on the player's psychology rather than the type of activity itself. One can be motivated to have fun not only in leisure activities but in some cases in necessary activities as well. A literature professor, say, may have fun using wordplay in the classroom or when writing poetry for publication. In the attitude sense, the activity that counts as play, such as in this case working as a professor, may be serious. On the other hand, one might agree to play a game in one's spare time reluctantly, with little chance of having fun, in which case one will not experience play in the attitude sense. If one does have fun playing a game, however, this will also count as play in the attitude sense, and not only in that sense but also in the activity sense.

In the activity sense, what counts as play depends not on the player's attitude but on the type of activity itself—sports and games, for instance. One plays hockey whether one does so for recreational fun or as a serious professional vying for the Stanley Cup. In the activity sense of play, it is impossible to play serious activities, like being a professor or any other type of employment, however much fun one might have doing it, that is, however much it may count as play in the attitude sense.

One can, however, play *at* serious activities—and this reflects the third sense, the acting sense of play—when one pretends to do them, as an actor does, rather than really doing something. Think of kids playing house. This kind of play, make-believe or playacting, implies both an attitudinal component and an activity component. To make believe is to knowingly act *as if* something unreal is real. The child playing house knows she isn't really married or going to work or doing chores. Likewise, I can't pretend to be a professor, since I am a professor, but I can pretend to be another professor, such as the lauded and much better-known Bertrand Russell, for I am not Bertrand Russell. Even a real war hero like Audie Murphy, when portraying himself in a movie (*To Hell and Back*), is still acting on screen pretending to do things he already actually did.

We should keep in mind these three different senses of play as we proceed, play as fun, play as participation, and play as make-believe, which help us coordinate different aspects of play on Huizinga's theory. Huizinga summarizes these characteristics as follows:

> Summing up the formal characteristics of play we might call it a free activity standing quite consciously outside "ordinary" life as being "not serious," but at the same time absorbing the player intensely and utterly. It is an activity connected with no material interest, and no profit can be gained by it. It proceeds within its own proper boundaries of time and space according to fixed rules and in an orderly manner. It promotes the formation of social groupings which tend to surround themselves with secrecy and to stress their difference from the common world by disguise or other means. (13)

We will expand on each of these in turn, anchored in Huizinga's analysis but adding detail to help explain certain important facets that might otherwise be ignored.

1. To say that play is free is to emphasize that it is voluntary, chosen. Play is not forced activity, but something the player elects to do. One can, of course, be forced to engage in play in the activity sense. One could play chess at gunpoint despite never having enjoyed the game and lacking any desire to play. Thus what is emphasized here is the attitude rather than participatory sense of an activity that qualifies as play. External agents or circumstances may "force" you to do something you don't want to do (although you could, in principle, refuse), but they can't force you to have fun doing it. At most they can incentivize the forced player pretending to have fun.

2. Just as play's voluntary character is in line with leisure's electivity, so too is the notion that play stands apart from ordinary life as something special. It is in that sense transcendent. Play in its robust sense, like leisure, is different from work, chores, school, and other activities that count most of the time for many people as ordinary or mundane in a neutral or pejorative sense. Such activities tend to be dull rather than exciting, the norm rather than the exception. This is not just part of the appropriate description of play, of what makes it play at all, but also part of its value, of what makes it worthwhile. Play is special insofar as it distinguishes itself from ordinary life in the mind of the player and in fact.

3. The absorbing nature of play is something it may share with some forms of work but in a rather different way. In play, when it is going well, one may get caught up in it, as with work. Time flies in that one becomes attentionally absorbed in the play at hand, just as certain work projects can require intense concentration. In play, however, the intense focus on it and relative inattention to the passage of time are *not* the results of the requirements of the task at hand and the effort to perform it, but rather come much more naturally because of sheer enjoyment, again, that is, when play is going well. This can happen with certain kinds of particularly rewarding work, but in that case work becomes play in the attitude sense.

4. The absorbing quality of good play dovetails naturally with the motivation for playing at all. Like leisure, again, the motivation for play is intrinsic rather than instrumental. One plays for its own sake rather than for the sake of something else, though again instrumental motivations are also possible. Along with enjoying their salary, a professional athlete will ideally also have fun playing their sport. Thus play at heart is autotelic, done for its own sake (from *auto* for self and *telos* for purpose), but not inconsistent with instrumental ends, as with leisure yet again.

5. That play is limited by boundaries, some formal or structural, others psychological or biological, is also noteworthy. Playgrounds and sport areas have sometimes less, sometimes more precisely specified dimensions. Play ends when children are called in for supper, when the clock runs out in a game, or when players simply don't want to play anymore. At some point play and players alike are, as Huizinga says, "played out" (9). The necessity of such boundaries is implied by the special status and intrinsic motivation of play. Without limits, play cannot be special or distinct from ordinary life. Unlimited play is no longer ludically distinguishable. Unlimited play is play no longer.

6. The cohesive function of play in forming and solidifying playgroups is a complex, double-edged phenomenon. On the positive side, playgroups tend to become tightly bonded, giving members a sense of identity and belonging. But because play is special to those in the playgroup, it tends toward exclusivity. Outsiders may be barred from rather than welcomed into the group, or seen as lesser for not being part of the group. Insiders likewise may be unfairly subjected to collective norms, expectations of group conformity irrespective of individual choice or

wellbeing. Think of the more abusive kinds of hazing rituals in some sport subcultures.

Culture as Play

Having seen Huizinga's account of play, we can now engage his view of its pivotal importance in human culture. Huizinga does not see play as an exclusively human phenomenon, by any means, and explicitly acknowledges it as part of what we have in common with non-human animals (1). But whereas play is rooted in natural impulses shared by human and other creatures alike, Huizinga sees the expression of play in human culture to be not so much continuous with non-human animals as distinctive, and not as local but pervasive. That is, as Huizinga holds play to be the basis of human culture itself, there should be discernible elements of play in all corners of human culture. This naturally includes not only obvious cultural manifestations of play, from pastime games to spectacle sports, but also, paradoxically, serious cultural domains that do not appear to be playful in any sense. If, furthermore, we can find elements of play in such serious domains, that would, from the outside, almost seem to undermine their legitimacy. Huizinga is indeed quite clear that there are elements of play even in the most serious parts of human culture, where the play element has receded into a solemn "ritual act" (20). We might be right to take such cultural domains seriously, but we are wrong sometimes to take them too seriously or to deny the significant elements of play that remain.

To illustrate his claim, Huizinga mentions various serious cultural domains in which there seems no place for anything like a play element. The key to understanding Huizinga here, I gather, is to imagine taking a step back from the culture and observing it as if one is an outsider. Of course, this is easier to do with cultures other than one's own, since by default one is in fact an outsider. From such a perspective, elements of play may be discernible even in serious cultural domains such as literature, religion, and the law. Even where literary works deal with fundamental, even existential problems of human existence, it is typically in the form of fiction, a kind of make-believe, not to mention the literal wordplay of poets. As serious as religion is as a source of spiritual meaning, its rituals and costumes—from an outsider's point of view—may appear arbitrary, even silly, though this does not necessarily compromise its solemnity. As Huizinga puts it, "[t]he ritual act, or an important part of it, will always remain within the play category, but in this seeming subordination the recognition of its holiness is not lost" (27). Likewise, in a court of law, even in a murder trial, there are deliberately dramatic elements and seemingly arbitrary customs: robes, gavels, wigs in some cases, special places and ceremonies for conducting the adversarial contest between prosecution and defence, and so on. Again, it is not that these domains are not serious—and, indeed, Huizinga problematizes the play/seriousness distinction (5)—but rather that serious as they are, they inevitably contain elements of play revealed as such in the possibility of appearing arbitrary or silly from an outsider's perspective.

Even from an insider's perspective, various cultural manifestations of play might appear odd or unappealing to some people, however much other people might be invested in them. These people are not cultural but rather subcultural outsiders. Consider contests, ostensibly different kinds of competitive play competition, whether sports, reality TV shows, beauty pageants, what have you. These contests are not always easy to categorize, as in the case of bodybuilding, which some believe qualifies as a sport, as a game of physical skill, and others believe to be a pageant, a competitive display of built bodies. Either way, many people don't see the point of sports or pageants, and among those who are drawn to certain types of contest, others often seem pointless or silly and their followers peculiar. As varieties of physical contest, sports range from player-centred recreational forms to viewer-centred elite forms exhibited in professional leagues and the Olympics. In all its forms, such contests remain play at heart even if this is more evident in recreational sport than elite sport. Someone playing pickup soccer on the weekend is more obviously at play than a top player vying for the World Cup championship. Although we can indeed take sport too seriously—think of enraged parents at children's games or pathologically obsessed fans of professional teams—in such contests the play element, again, has receded, and so is still present despite being difficult to discern.

In contrast to those who embrace play—lightly, rightly, or too tightly—we find the figure of the spoilsport. Huizinga defines the spoilsport in terms of three essential characteristics: they refuse either (1) to play or (2) even pretend to play, thus (3) ruining play by shattering the illusory play-world (11). A common example is the petulant child who doesn't want to play anymore or at all and so selfishly takes their ball home, preventing others from playing further. Spoilsports are typically people behaving badly, as with the refrain from *South Park*'s Eric Cartman, "Screw you guys! I'm going home." One interesting wrinkle here, for Huizinga, is the notion that society is "much more lenient" to cheats, those who break the rules of a game, than spoilsports (11). Why would this be? Since cheating is intended to be hidden, cheats are still pretending to play fairly, and so despite their immorality help maintain, as honest players do, the illusory play-world. By refusing to play at all, however, spoilsports threaten the very existence of the play-world itself, ruining play for others.

So depicted, the spoilsport seems a particularly nasty, unsympathetic character for ruining play for others. However, the matter isn't that simple, as there are at least two respects in which spoilsports may be sympathetic and morally praiseworthy. Remember that, for Huizinga, elements of play are to be found throughout the culture. One might be considered a spoilsport simply by refusing to go along with the group, by asserting one's independence in refusing to do just what the group wants, whether in the case of benign play that one simply doesn't want to participate in, or as taking a moral stance against a questionable or clearly immoral form of "cultural play." Some spoilsports, for Huizinga, are "innovators, prophets, conscientious objectors" (12), or we could add whistleblowers, people who call out unethical cultural attitudes and practices. Thus a Martin Luther King may be rightly described and justly praised as a spoilsport of racist culture. This means that the spoilsport's moral status is not a matter of ruining play but rather a consequence of the moral status of the play itself and the motivation for spoiling it.

PLAY AND LEISURE

Where the focus of Huizinga's analysis of play is decidedly social, the focus of Nash's analysis of play is more psychological. Likewise, where Huizinga does not, except in passing, Nash does explicitly connect his account of play to leisure. One of Nash's central concerns is what makes for better and worse forms of leisure, and it turns out that the key to better leisure is play. Indeed, for Nash play is what makes not only leisure but even work qualitatively better.

Nash situates his theory of play within a general account of human activity and activity generally as distinguishing living organisms from other things and for which we have an innate tendency. As Nash puts it, further, "[b]ecause of its strength and universality, the activity drive has important implications in the life and education of each of us" (83). Learning begins with random responses to stimuli, internal and external, and through trial and error become by degrees more subtle, complex, and orderly. In this way, activity grounds cognitive development, which on Nash's view proceeds in four stages (84–85). We begin at the observational level, sensing and responding to stimuli. Next, we move on to the exploratory level, where stimuli are not just experienced and responded to but sought by moving through the world. More sophisticated, then, is the investigatory level, where one begins to manipulate things in the world, though without understanding. Lastly, at the experimental level comes an understanding and testing of these various manipulations of stimuli involving the imagination and rudimentary theory.

Whereas many activities marked by cognitive maturity are, as we know, motivated extrinsically, play is, as Nash says, "an activity that carries its own drive" (82). We naturally associate play with leisure, and to the extent that work may be unfulfilling, the importance of play and leisure will come to the fore. But for Nash, again, play is what makes for rewarding experience in not just leisure but work as well. The play impulse can be stifled, of course, often by work that "becomes mechanical, routine, and dull and no longer challenging," work that is "drudgery" rather than "creative" (Nash 82). The lack of play in leisure can be a problem too, in which case one has not fulfilling leisure experiences but mere recreation, even dissipation and destruction, activities potentially harmful to oneself or to society. We should note here Nash's emphasis on and possible bias toward active leisure and creative play rather than forms tending more to the passive, receptive, and appreciative. This will become clear when we come to Nash's leisure hierarchy below.

Before that, however, we should consider the possibility raised by Nash's account of a play ethic standing as both antithetical and corrective to an extreme work ethic. In a crucial sense, value here is seen as afforded not by work, for its own or even leisure's sake, but by play itself to the benefit of leisure and work alike. From a work ethic perspective, play seems childish, unproductive, and bad. From a play ethic perspective, however, play seems not childish but child*like*, not productive but creative, and not bad but good, thus partly denying the work ethic's characterization of play and partly inverting its values. A work ethic can value play as recreation, as facilitating work, of course, as a play ethic can value work in service of play. In this sense, at least, there are implied exceptions to each view.

Recalling that Nash is interested in accounting for qualitative differences among different kinds of leisure activities, and doing so in terms of play, consider his leisure hierarchy (Figure 6.1). In terms of leisure that is, all else being equal, positive, the lowest level is entertainment, mere amusement, where the purpose is escapism or merely killing time. At the next level up, one is not just distracting oneself or idly passing the time but participating on an emotional level. Consider the difference between casually watching an unremarkable movie and getting caught up and emotionally invested in an exceptional film. Better than merely emotional participation is active participation, for instance, the difference between watching a good game on television and playing the sport oneself. Best of all is participation that is not just active but also creative, the difference, say, between learning to perform a song someone else has written and actually writing a song yourself. The more passive and less creative the leisure activity, for Nash, the lower it ranks on the hierarchy, whereas the more active and creative it is, the higher it ranks. This leisure hierarchy stresses the vital role of play since it is in play that activity and creativity meet.

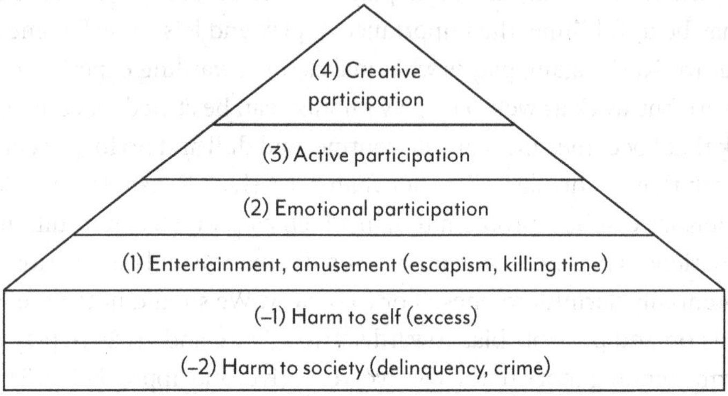

FIGURE 6.1 *Nash's leisure hierarchy*

Nash claims that having a selection of leisure activities from each level "may be good, but too many activities low on the scale are dulling, and in the end progress and development of the individual and the group are retarded" (89). This appeal to leisure's instrumental implications might seem curious, yet until now in this book little mention has been made of the potential negative consequences of some leisure activities. Activities that count for Nash as "less than zero" include those that harm the self and, worse, those that harm society. Think of the difference between someone who drinks socially (level 1), someone with a drinking problem (level -1), and someone who drives intoxicated (level -2). Worst of all, on this model, are dark leisure activities that constitute delinquency or crime, harmful to society at least and often also to the individual themselves.

There is little doubt that Nash's leisure hierarchy boasts a significant degree of plausibility. Most of us could probably benefit from trying to diversify our leisure activities along the lines Nash suggests. It would be remiss, however, not to mention certain complications arising from Nash's own interpretation as well as potential applications of his leisure hierarchy. This first consideration is twofold, and concerns the apparent failure of Nash's hierarchy to account for pluralism. Although Nash cautions us against too much low-level leisure to the detriment of high-level leisure, this probably doesn't apply to people, such as professional artists, who already have great and exhaustively demanding creative outlets in their jobs. It seems wrong to expect much if any active or creative leisure from those who may often be actively or creatively tapped out professionally, or who, whatever their jobs, find themselves far less suited to either performing or enjoying such creative endeavours. Another problem is categorization. Many people would consign graffiti, such as so-called tagging, to the second sublevel in the leisure hierarchy. However, some graffiti art has undeniable artistic merit and even social significance, as with Banksy, for instance. Such a graffiti artist may be seen to occupy, simultaneously, the very top and the very bottom of Nash's leisure hierarchy. The ultimate significance of these issues for Nash's account I will not address here.

CONCLUSION

Although, for our purposes, Huizinga and Nash provide the most relevant theories of play, I do not mean to give the impression that the philosophy of play is limited to these two thinkers. In some ways, indeed, we have barely scratched the surface of widespread and diverse philosophical interest in play. In Plato's *The Laws*, for instance, the best part of what human beings are is attributed to play, not because we are subjects of play, not because we do play, but because we are objects of play, specifically as "playthings" of the gods (803). More down to earth, philosophers of sport are interested in play both because sports are physical games that we play and because the right balance between playful and competitive would seem ideal for athletes whose pursuit of excellence exhibits ethical virtue no less than physical prowess. Thus in the next chapter we turn to the nature of games, physical and otherwise, which are sometimes considered leisure activities par excellence.

QUESTIONS FOR CONSIDERATION

- Is all culture a form of play on some level, or are there exceptions? Should one ever play when engaged in serious activities?
- Is there such a thing as a play ethic? How might a play ethic and a leisure ethic differ from each other and from the more familiar work ethic?
- Whose theory of play gets at the heart of leisure better, Huizinga's or Nash's? Why do you find that theory more insightful?
- Besides an activity drive, do we also have a "passivity drive"? If so, what does this imply about the relationship between play and leisure?
- Does Nash's theory exhibit a bias toward more active and more creative forms of leisure, or is this indicative of an objective difference in value?
- What sort of distribution among Levels 1–4 in Nash's hierarchy would be ideal? Does it depend on the individual or context?

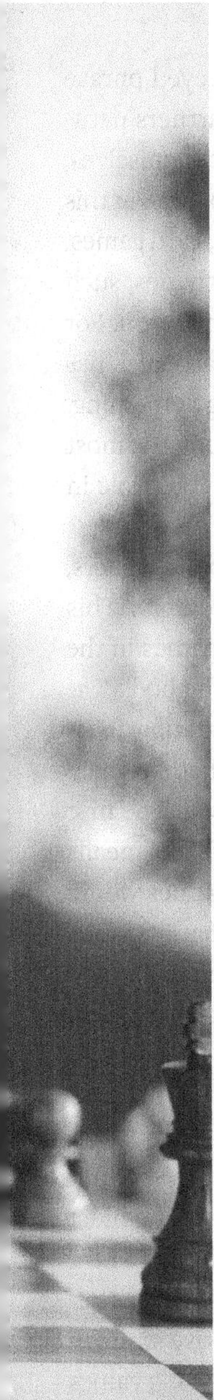

CHAPTER 7

Games We Play

To further enlarge our understanding of leisure, in this chapter we address the philosophy of games, in particular the theory of games—what they are, and why they matter—proposed by Bernard Suits. This theory is arguably the most robust and successful philosophical analysis of the subject, though it is not without its critics. Suits's theory has been criticized as an account of games themselves and, as applied, of the importance of games in a good life and their alleged central role in an ideal one. In Suits's view, a utopian existence for human beings would maximize leisure by spending most of one's time and energy playing games.

INTRODUCTION

When referring to leisure activities, we often employ the hackneyed phrase "fun and games." The word "fun" certainly suggests play, and partners naturally with games and other leisure activities. The nature of games themselves, though, is something we have yet to explore, and this is what we explore in this chapter. There are various types of games, of course: board games, card games, sports, and so on, which we find among various other leisure activities, such as watching television, reading, chatting over coffee, traveling, and so on. For many people, playing games, not generally but certain games in particular, has a singular prominence. Note too that when it comes to watching something, idly or with a keen interest, games and particularly sports are among the most popular for many people. In other words, games play perhaps a larger role in many people's leisure than we might initially think.

There are various definitions of games proposed by different philosophers, but none has achieved such distinction as that offered by Bernard Suits. This theory has, for one illustration, become the canonical theory of games in the philosophy of sport. Suits's fullest articulation of his theory, in the book *The Grasshopper: Games, Life and Utopia*, originally published in 1978 and now in its third edition, is widely regarded as a philosophical classic. This theory, which will occupy our attention throughout this chapter, is two-pronged. The first prong consists in a theoretical definition of games, specifically what it means to play a game. The second prong is a theory of the central role games would play, in Suits's view, in a utopian existence. The implication is that, if games would be the central activity in an ideal life, then we should make enough room for games in less than ideal lives like ours. We should, in other words, not deny games their rightful place either in our lives or in our esteem.

DEFINING GAMES

Since Suits's definition of games is not the only one, though it is the most prominent, by way of contrast consider the definition of games offered by Loy: "any playful competition whose outcome is determined by physical skill, strategy, or chance employed singly or in combination" (39). A comparative strength of this definition is the inclusion of a finer-grained taxonomy, analyzing games generally into the subclasses of games of skill (e.g., weightlifting), games of strategy (e.g., chess), and games of chance (e.g., roulette). A related strength is that besides relatively "pure" cases, other games blend these elements. Card games such as poker blend strategy and chance in determining who will win or lose. Winners in team sports like football are typically jointly determined by physical skill and strategy. Still, the definition has drawbacks. Some games are cooperative rather than competitive. Likewise, some high-level games are so serious as to nullify the sense that those who play them are doing so playfully. Relatedly, without explicit mention of rules, it is not clear how this definition is meant to distinguish games from play.

Accounting for the often solemn seriousness of games is one of Suits's objectives. Denying the potential seriousness of games, Suits says, "is very much like saying to the Pope that Catholicism is just religion, to Beethoven that the quartets are just music, or to Muhammad Ali that boxing is just a sport" ("Elements" 64). Accordingly, Suits defines games in terms of their structural features and including only those psychological elements strictly necessary for those structural features. One thing worth noting here is that Suits takes as his paradigm case of games not a board game or card game but the physical contest of a footrace. When he says that "the elements of sport are essentially—although perhaps not totally—the same as the elements of game" ("Elements" 48), Suits leaves little doubt about the central importance of physical games to his account of games generally. Indeed, Suits marshals his definition of games with an eye to establishing a definition of sport. This focus on physical games gives some leverage to certain objections to Suits's theory to be discussed after recapping the theory itself.

In identifying different elements of game play to assemble into his definition, Suits distinguishes idiosyncratic purposes in playing a game from the object of the game itself. Thus one could participate in a footrace for various purposes—to have fun, to kill time, as exercise, for camaraderie's sake, what have you—but the one purpose that cannot be avoided in playing the game is the object of the game itself, in the case of a footrace crossing the finish line first. Whatever one's further purpose may be, fun, fitness, or friendship, none of these is essential to, and all of them depend on, the prescribed object of the game itself. For Suits, however, the object of a game is what he calls its prelusory goal—*ludus* being Latin for play or game—which is "*a specific achievable state of affairs*" identifiable apart from any game itself and without appealing to any game rules ("Elements" 50). Where the lusory goal of a footrace is to cross the finish line first, the *pre*lusory goal is to cross a certain line (e.g., one you draw in the sand) first, which in a footrace is specified by the rules as the finish line. Thus for Suits the first essential element of games is the presence of a prelusory goal.

As all games have objects, so too do they have rules. Suits lays great stress on the importance of rules for games. Rules, of course, distinguish the boundaries of acceptable actions in games, separating what is permissible, the lusory means, from what is impermissible. Suits illustrates with the examples of a footrace and soccer: in a footrace, one is may not cut across the infield ("Elements" 49), and in soccer, a "player may use foot or head, but not hand ... to achieve that state of affairs wherein the ball is in the goal" ("Elements" 51). For Suits, however, the rules do not just distinguish what you can from what you can't do in a game, they constitute the game, defining it. Suits speaks here of the constitutive rules of a game, those that must be followed if one is to play the game at all ("Elements" 51). In playing soccer, for instance, I cannot pick up the ball and run downfield football style. Using hands more than soccer allows would sometimes be a more efficient means, just as cutting across the infield in a footrace would be, but that is how constitutive rules work. They rule out more efficient "illusory" means in favour of less efficient lusory means. Thus two identifiable game elements come together here, lusory means as circumscribed by constitutive rules.

Suits identifies one more crucial element of playing games, which he calls the lusory attitude. In playing games, one accepts the arbitrary constraints imposed by the constitutive rules simply and solely because one wants to play the game, because it is those arbitrary constraints that, as constitutive rules, make the game possible (Suits, "Elements" 54). In contrast to many other types of rules outside a game context, which have a presumption of independent justification and so are not arbitrary, game rules are completely arbitrary *except* as structuring internally desirable play. Legal and moral rules against theft, for instance, are not game rules, because they have independent justifications as part of what it means to live in a civilized society, part of the social contract that makes living in society rational. We typically avoid committing theft because we recognize its wrongness or, failing that, a wish to avoid punishment when the reward is inevitably not worth the risk.

Apart from a game, however, accepting truly arbitrary constraints, those that serve no further purpose whatsoever, would be irrational rather than rational. One refrains from picking up the ball in soccer because one wants to play soccer, and from cutting across the infield because one wants to run the race. If one refrains from such activities because, oddly, the possibility does not occur to one, if one avoids more efficient means out of ignorance rather than knowledge, one lacks a lusory attitude, and so, in Suits's terms, is not playing the game. If one wants to get to the other side of the racetrack, and there is no reason not to take the most direct route across the infield, it would be irrational not to do so. What would be irrational in everyday life, accepting arbitrary constraints of imposed inefficiency, becomes the very hallmark of game player psychology.

We are now in a position to assemble the elements of Suits's philosophical definition of playing games into that very definition. On Suits's view, playing a game means meeting the following necessary and sufficient conditions, each being necessary, all a guarantee: "To play a game is to attempt to achieve a specific state of affairs (*prelusory goal*), using only means permitted by the rules (*lusory means*), where the rules prohibit more efficient in favour of less efficient means (*constitutive rules*), and where such rules are accepted just because they make possible such activity (*lusory attitude*)" ("Elements" 55). Suits then packs this complete definition into the following compressed definition: "Playing a game is the voluntary attempt to overcome unnecessary obstacles" ("Elements" 55). If an obstacle is necessary, or if the effort to overcome it is forced rather than chosen, one is not playing a game. Jumping over a hurdle in fleeing for one's life is not playing a game, but doing so in a race is.

Before moving on to criticisms of Suits's theory of games, we will briefly consider his definition of sport, which builds on the foundation of his definition of games, the latter again having since become the canonical theory of games in the philosophy of sport. As Suits identifies four necessary and sufficient conditions for games, so too does he identify four necessary and sufficient conditions for sport. Distinct from other games, sports are games of skill rather than chance, where that skill is essentially physical—strategy isn't enough—with a following of players and other interested parties that is wide rather than local and stable rather than faddish (Suits, "Elements" 58–60). If we came up with our own unique game of physical skill, that would not become a sport, in Suits's view, until and unless it became widely played and stood the test of time, though where to draw the line in either case seems difficult.

CRITIQUES OF SUITS

There are various critiques of Suits's definition of games, even among those who readily acknowledge the significance of the theory they target. One type of criticism is to raise potential counterexamples to Suits's commitment to all games having prelusory goals. Other criticisms focus on different dimensions of Suits's account of constitutive rules. Some games appear to lack constitutive rules as characterized by Suits, and the wide scope of constitutive rules as set by Suits seems to be too broad. Others picture the identity of games less in terms of the rules themselves and more in terms of how those rules are interpreted and applied. Still others see the problem as one with such philosophical definitions generally. It could be that games and other such cultural types cannot be defined along the lines envisioned by Suits. Others, too, criticize Suits's theory of sport, predicated on his theory of games, as institutionalized rather than in terms of the activity or practice itself. We will see how someone may reply to these objections on Suits's behalf, as well as acknowledging the theoretical value of his theory irrespective of such critiques.

All games have lusory goals, or objects, states of affairs the achievement of which will determine the winner, at least in games that have winners.[1] But Suits makes the further claim that such objects are prelusorily describable, that is, without appeal to the rules. But consider the possible counterexample of chess. The lusory goal of chess is to checkmate the opponent. But trying to describe checkmate without appeal to the rules turns out to be extraordinarily difficult, if not impossible (Schneider and Butcher 39). What is checkmate? Checkmate means the king is under attack and there is no legal way to nullify it. But that is *not* a prelusory description, since "king," "attack," "legal," and "nullify" are defined by the rules of chess. Trying to reduce such terms even further, down to the level of a prelusory description, is hardly a straightforward task.

Similar considerations apply to videogames, although here the problem is further compounded by an apparent glitch in Suits's concept of constitutive rules, at least as applying to videogames. Recall first that, for Suits, the prelusory goal of a race may be described as crossing a designated line first, the rules then defining it as the finish line. But think of a race game played on a computer. The virtual world of a computer game depends on the program itself, the code, the rules. In real life you can draw a line in the sand or with tape without rules, but in a videogame "there is no game-independently drawable line a first crossing of which can constitute the prelusory goal, just as there is no actual space in which one is able to draw the line" (Holt, "Virtual Domains" 10). Unlike the real world, the existence of a videogame's virtual world depends on the rules defining it. Relatedly, for Suits a game's constitutive rules, such as the one prohibiting cutting across the infield in a footrace, are *breakable* rules that players honour, since they want to play, as a matter of choice. The rules of a videogame, however, are set by the programming. In playing a videogame, then, one does not choose to attempt to overcome unnecessary obstacles. One is rather forced to follow the rules, which makes them more like natural laws, which must be obeyed, than game rules as conceived by Suits (Holt, "Virtual Domains" 10). Thus videogames pose a double challenge to Suits's theory of games.

In contrast to such counterexamples, other critiques focus on Suits painting the constitutiveness of games with a very wide brush. Suits does admit that, in addition to constitutive rules, games also have rules of skill such as

1 Perhaps rally games, where one tries to keep play going indefinitely, do not have winners, since rallies inevitably come to an end.

"Keep your eye on the ball," which concern what it means to play well rather than what it means to play at all ("Elements" 52). Even so, the notion that the rules of a game are mostly constitutive may be guilty of overreach. To illustrate constitutive rules in another context, Suits mentions the offside rules in football and hockey ("Tricky Triad" 5–6), though we could add soccer and rugby as well. But this kind of rule more intuitively seems to be of a different type than constitutive rules or rules of skill, which Meier calls regulative rules (20). The difference is important. If it is a constitutive rule, then a player who accidentally goes offside is no longer playing the game. If it is a regulative rule, however, we get a more intuitive result: the player going offside has not failed to play the game at all but failed to play it legally.[2] This is the more plausible interpretation.

Another concern, arising in various forms, is that Suits's formalism, the definition of games in terms of their rules, seems to yield implausible implications, especially in light of alternative views on the relationship between rules and game integrity. Suppose, for instance, that what defines a game is not the rules themselves but how those rules are interpreted and applied. The logic for doing so will be tied to the rules in one way or another but not determined by them. Certain forms of rule-breaking will be seen as consistent with maintaining game integrity, whereas others will not. Conventionalists believe that this logic is arbitrary, a matter of the cultural or subcultural conventions governing how to interpret and apply rules. Thus officials in one region may interpret and apply rules differently than those in other regions. Interpretivists, on the other hand, see the logic as more closely tied to the rules themselves and holding constant across various sport subcultures, as it is the best interpretation of the rules that should govern their proper application rather than simply a matter of how we do things. Here there is a greater claim to objectivity and far less room for pluralism, though overall both views offer powerful challenges to Suitsian formalism.

Yet another challenge targets the whole project of providing such definitions for philosophically interesting types like justice, beauty, and games. Where such definitions purport to reveal the essence of a kind of thing, anti-essentialists hold that succeeding in this project will prove impossible, unnecessary, or unhelpful. We first encountered this concern in Chapter 1 in connection with my proposed definition of leisure. For Wittgenstein, who popularized the anti-essentialist view, what holds the category of games together is not

2 Along with constitutive (*what*) rules and regulative (*how*) rules, Meier posits auxiliary (*who*) rules, which govern eligibility (18).

some underlying essence like the voluntary attempt to overcome unnecessary obstacles, but rather, with nothing common and peculiar to the class, a set of family resemblances, "a complicated network of similarities overlapping and criss-crossing" (§ 66). When he proposed his definition, Suits was certainly familiar with Wittgenstein's use of games as his paradigm case of things that cannot be defined, and although the original articulations of Suits's view do not directly confront such anti-essentialism, the positive arguments they provide deliberately flout the anti-essentialist stance.

One last criticism of Suits's view targets not his definition of game but his definition of sport as a game of physical skill with a wide and stable following. Stipulating that such a following is necessary for a physical game to qualify as sport is an institutional requirement, one implying that sport is a social kind rather than a kind of activity or practice, distinguishing them from games that are not also sports. Some sport philosophers resist any institutional requirement for sport. For one example, Meier observes that sports like jai alai and hurling are so geographically limited—Miami/Cuba and Ireland, respectively—that their followings are local rather than wide, yet there is no good reason to deny them sport status (16). I think we should resist, furthermore, such institutional requirements as would unfairly exclude from the sport class various Indigenous sports, such as those in the Inuit games as well as precolonial lacrosse. In general, informal pickup games of any given sport—provide your own examples—seem no less plausible instances than official league games (Meier 17). Like non-sport games, then, and more than many other types of leisure, what makes something a sport seems to be the physical game it is, not the institutional context in which it may but need not occur.

Despite these substantial criticisms of Suits's theoretical perspective on games and sports, there are different responses that could be made, and several that already have been made, on his behalf. The headline here is that Suits's theory remains of vital importance to our understanding of games. Owing to limited space, however, I will enumerate these responses but briefly.

1. Although describing a prelusory goal for chess is difficult, I suggest it is not impossible. Consider that the chess convention when one is checkmated is to lay the king down on its side. We might describe the prelusory goal of chess as the specific state of affairs where the tallest piece, or the one with the cross, is on its side (Holt, "Virtual Domains" 11), since these are the characteristics that nominally distinguish the king from other pieces.

2. With videogames, similarly, we could "[c]onsider a general strategy that takes the lusory goal of winning or what it means to win in lusory terms and reduces it to some nominal description that may be identified as the prelusory goal" (Holt, "Virtual Domains" 11). Where winning is a matter of the highest score, this reduces to the prelusory goal of having, say, the highest number beside one's name. Likewise, the fact that many videogames include cheat codes suggests compliance with Suits's concept of constitutive rules (Holt, "Virtual Domains" 11). Not availing themselves of a cheat code, a gamer is voluntarily attempting to overcome unnecessary obstacles.

3. Although Suits is probably guilty of overreach in specifying the scope of constitutive rules within games, this does not necessarily invalidate his formalist interpretation of game rules. In the case of a regulative rule, such as going offside, officials have clear procedures for reestablishing game integrity, say, with a whistle and loss of possession. With auxiliary rule violations, such as taking banned performance enhancers, athletes are stripped of their merely nominal achievements as if they had never competed at all.

4. Objections to formalism have been found persuasive by many sport philosophers. However, the formalist seems to get something right about the relationship between game integrity and how players should honour the rules. Even if certain rules could be broken without undermining game integrity, when this happens it is nonetheless *as if* the rule-breaker has nullified the game, since they have irrevocably departed from what it ideally should be. Despite the venerable distinction between fact and value, between "is" and "ought," the norm-governed practices of games seem tailormade to bridge this gap.

5. Even if anti-essentialists are right to charge essentialists with metaphysical prejudice in favour of such theoretical definitions, it seems no less reasonable to charge anti-essentialists with the opposite prejudice that such definitions are pointless if not impossible. The fair solution would seem to be taking general cultural terms on a case-by-case basis and seeing whether a worthy definition is forthcoming. Suits's theory of games flies in the face of denying such definitions altogether as a matter of principle.

6. A defender of Suits's theory of sport could observe, against activity- or practice-based objectors, that institutional versions of sport are, really, the core examples of sport that make it interesting both to viewers and theoretically. If non-institutional instances are of interest because they bear a structural resemblance to core cases (i.e., by following the same rules, more or less), perhaps they do count as sport by dint of exhibiting similar patterns of activity as core cases. Even newly minted sports such as mixed martial arts seem to have been mere curiosities until they achieved institutional equilibrium.

Whatever merit we might find in these efforts to shore up Suits's account, any remaining flaws will not necessarily undermine its theoretical usefulness, which seems all but undeniable. For instance, the compressed definition of game playing offers a useful means of discussing the possibility that there could be nonhuman game players, such as horses in equine sports, which seem sometimes to so qualify (Holt, "Horses as Players" 456). Likewise, as we have seen, Suits's theory suggests provocative facets of interpreting virtual games, whether videogames or chess, which can of course be played on a computer, and contrasting them with games of other kinds.

UTOPIAN GAMES

The second part of Suits's influential take on games, connecting more obviously with our understanding of leisure, is his view that, in an ideal world, a utopian existence where work is unnecessary and leisure is king, people would spend most of their waking life playing games. According to Suits, then, it is games that constitute not just one form of leisure but the best kind of leisure possible.

Suits's vision of utopia is expressed toward the end of *The Grasshopper*: "game playing performs a crucial role in delineating that [utopian] ideal—a role which cannot be performed by any other activity, and without which an account of the ideal is either incomplete or impossible" (149). Suits is explicit that the book's eponymous hero is the very same one "whom Aesop made everlastingly famous as the model of improvidence" (*Grasshopper* 21), in contrast to the industrious ant from the same fable. Whereas the ant was originally intended to model the virtue of a work ethic as a safeguard against times of precarity, Suits inverts these values insofar as an ideal existence implies a leisure ethic, complete security in plenty rather than insecurity over precarity. In Suits's utopia, people would be "engaged only in those activities which they value intrinsically" (*Grasshopper* 149). Although ungamified play is also valued intrinsically, we humans seem to find more rewarding and more meaningful certain activities that are both goal-directed and structured—think prelusory goal and constitutive rules—that is, games, whereas ungamified play is either aimless, unstructured, or both.

The details of such a utopia are somewhat sketchy and hard to imagine. Suits's utopian vision includes the elimination of all necessary work, everyone's material needs being met by automation or telepathy (*Grasshopper* 150). No competition would be necessary either, since all goods and services would exist or be created instantly to meet whatever demand arose. Nor would there be any psychological or social problems, since these derive from scarcity-based conflict in less-than-ideal worlds, and there is no cause for such conflict in an ideal world. As far as romantic love goes, for example, Suits states, curiously, that in his utopia "sexual partners are every bit as accessible as yachts and diamonds" (*Grasshopper* 150). It certainly gives one pause, this notion that interpersonal relationships would *ideally* be characterized by such fungibility, such indifferent interchangeability, rather than intrinsically valuing unique people for their inherent specialness.

In utopia, then, meaning would not be found in morality, art, or science, or in friendship or love, as we currently understand these pursuits and relationships, since the usually instrumental motivations for them, from being productive to being validated, are not in effect (*Grasshopper* 151–53). As difficult—and as desirable—as it may be to grasp this ideal as Suits envisions it, it might be easier if we consider it along lines analogous to biblical Eden or different concepts of heaven, where real-world concerns about practical matters simply don't apply. Whether such visions are as desirable as their proponents claim is, for present purposes, a matter best left aside.

If we accept that the meaning we attach to morality, art, science, friendship, and love applies in the real world but not the utopian world, what remains? What, in other words, is there to do in utopia? The only plausible answer, for Suits, is games. There may be some room for aimless or unstructured play in Suits's utopia, but the best and predominant form of leisure would be playing games. Utopian games would include not only games we know—board games, sports, and so on—but also gamified activities that are, in the real world, instrumentally motivated, but which may be intrinsically enjoyable to certain utopians. Suits posits hypothetical utopians John Striver and William Seeker, who enjoy the activities of carpentry and science, respectively, despite their utopian uselessness (*Grasshopper* 156–58). Instead of instantly having something built or knowing some fact, Striver enjoys the process of building things with his own hands, while Seeker enjoys discovering things for himself. By opting out of more efficient means of building and discovering things, Striver and Seeker have gamified, as their preferred forms of leisure, activities that otherwise have no place in Suits's utopia.

As far-fetched and sketchily detailed as Suits's utopia is, there are different sources of concern regarding whether such a way of life is sustainable, even setting aside that the automated systems may break down or the telepathic powers wear out. Suits himself worries that the utopians might eventually see games as no less empty than aimless and unstructured play (*Grasshopper* 59–60). J.S. Russell argues that idleness would not only rival games for the attention of Suits's utopians but would come to be seen as preferable ("Idleness in Utopia" 398). Granting plausibility to Russell's point, even if Suits is right that utopians would be largely concerned with games, this does not necessarily mean that they would spend too much of their time *playing* games. The problem, as I see it, is that people are often more inclined to *watch* others play games—sports are a prime example—than to play games themselves. One could well imagine Suits's utopians preferring to idly watch others play games, an audience in search of a spectacle, with some utopians persuaded or coerced to perform for the idle amusement of others. Call this "the no player problem." The implicit assumption is that we are more inclined to passivity than activity, which is plausible enough. The result is hardly utopian and more dystopian, or else a throwback to ancient times. Looming large is the spectre of limiting the freedom of some to enhance the leisure of many. In the next chapter, then, we turn to leisure and freedom.

QUESTIONS FOR CONSIDERATION

- Can Suits's theory of games be defended from the criticisms discussed?
- Which of your favourite leisure activities are games, and which are not? What does this suggest about the importance of games in leisure?
- Is academia a kind of game? Or being a good person? Is life itself a kind of game?
- What games would you play in Suits's utopia? Would you engage in any other activities that do not really count as games?
- Does Suits's utopia make sense? Does it have potential problems other than those discussed? Do you think you would like it there?
- In describing everyone's needs being met in utopia, does Suits confuse fungibility (e.g., *someone* being available) and individuality (e.g., some *one* being available)?

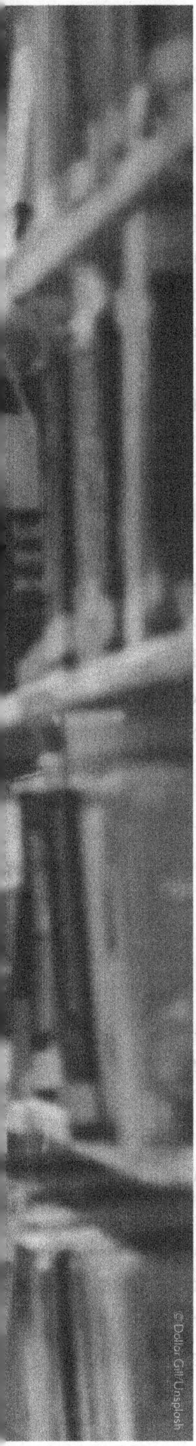
© Dollar Gill/Unsplash

CHAPTER 8
Freedom in Leisure

Leisure connotes freedom from obligation and doing what one wants. It is in this sense individualistic, as different people will want to do different things. This view, however, sits uncomfortably with the notion that some leisure is unworthy or badly spent, that one is never completely free from moral obligation, or that one can benefit from leisure education to make more informed and ultimately better leisure choices. Still, leisure seems to be the last bastion of liberty where, so long as we do no harm to others, our choices are subject to no one's approval but our own. In this regard, following Wes Cooper, the good of leisure—as leisure—derives from an individual's current, fully considered, self-directed, end-oriented preferences. Here, good leisure is good for the individual leisure-goer.

INTRODUCTION

Our ordinary concept of leisure suggests an intimate, but not necessarily straightforward, relationship with freedom. In Chapter 1 we saw that a negative concept of leisure, as freedom from work and other obligations, is thin compared with a positive concept of what leisure is for, that is, of what we choose to do with it. Taking up this theme again in a somewhat different form, our ordinary concept of freedom is negative, as freedom *from* something undesirable. But this negative concept needs supplementation by a positive concept of freedom *for* something desirable or the freedom *to* do something desirable, which itself requires theoretical elaboration.

There is something of a paradox lurking here, however. As much as leisure intuitively seems to be the one domain, if there is only one, where individual freedom should reign, we often criticize other people for their leisure choices, for doing leisure wrong. In Western leisure generally, we might be free of all other obligations, but not those imposed by morality and the law. We can't engage in leisure that harms others, and there are imposed limits even on potential harms to oneself, although whether there should be is a matter of debate. Likewise, in Asian, African, and Indigenous cultures, individual freedom may take a back seat to collective concerns, practices, and traditions. Given our sense of how individual leisure is so often wasted, and culturally relative besides, we may consider the question of whether, and to what extent, leisure itself is justified.

THE JUSTIFICATION QUESTION

Again, the notion that leisure should need justification seems odd indeed, whether we mean leisure as a way of being or leisure as a subject worthy of scholarly inquiry. It is, as we have seen, an excessive work ethic that makes leisurely pursuits, beyond their recreational value in renewing us for work again, seem unworthy. From such a perspective, too, if leisure seems frivolous, so would taking it seriously as a topic for academic study, whether in the context of leisure studies itself or as an applied field for other related disciplines such as psychology and, as here, philosophy. But if Aristotle is right that we work for the sake of leisure, if a leisure ethic expresses some part of what makes life worth living, then that would seem to be all the justification we could ask for vis-à-vis leisure and its study. If leisure is part of, or provides the means to, what makes life meaningful, it is for that reason alone justified both as a way of being and as a subject worthy of scholarly research.

Indeed, there is an important connection between leisure in life and leisure as subject matter in such a book as this. Consider not just the activity of leisure as contemplation but the higher-order, meta-activity of contemplating in leisure the nature of leisure itself. Such consideration of leisure in leisure is, furthermore, not just a matter of idle musing. Although many people are indeed employed in academia, the world of higher education, over and above vocational training, is itself a kind of leisure. Charles puts it quite succinctly: "leisure and education are linked at the semantic hip, school meaning leisure in Greek (*schole*) and Latin (*scola*). This link should not be attributed to a quirk of lexicographical evolution but to a fundamental interrelationship" (47). For instructors and students alike, the epitome of this perspective is to be found, as we have seen, in the vision of a liberal education. In the unique case of leisure studies in higher education, "we have found leisure in order to discuss leisure" (Charles 47). Thus at some point in higher education the pursuit of knowledge comes to consider itself reflexively, with leisure both root and flower, foundation and spire.

The question of justification remains, however, especially if one is concerned chiefly with social utility rather than individual liberty. We may ask ourselves the question, "Can the world be trusted with leisure?" (Goodale and Godbey 145), and the answer might not be obvious. In his essay "On Liberty and Leisure," Charles addresses this question in part by discussing the works of John Stuart Mill (1806–73), which severally may be taken to illustrate this tension between social utility and individual liberty, in the books *Utilitarianism* and *On Liberty*, respectively. To take social utility first, Mill is one of the prominent early exponents of utilitarianism, the moral theory that "actions are right in proportion as they tend to promote happiness, wrong as they tend to produce the reverse of happiness" (*Utilitarianism* 2.2). Here happiness means pleasure and the absence of pain. Morally appropriate actions, on this view, are those that maximize utility, as in the slogan "The greatest happiness for the greatest number." Such a principle provides moral guidelines for human actions in general, including constraints on leisure behaviour, as well as specific ethical guidelines for leisure professionals.

Figuring out what action to perform in a utilitarian framework is idealized as calculating—using what is often called the utilitarian calculus—which available option would maximize utility, would bring the most happiness into the world. The calculus takes various factors or "measures" into account to rank different pleasure outcomes of different actions. Of the following factors, the first seven were proposed by Mill's predecessor Jeremy Bentham (1748–1832) (4.4), the last by Mill himself (*Utilitarianism* 2.6). We will assume for now that the utilitarian principle is always in effect, no matter whether one is at work or leisure. After enumerating the factors, we will address certain concerns arising from this assumption.

» *Intensity*. All else being equal, a more intense pleasure is better than one less intense, and a less intense pain is better than one more intense.

» *Duration*. All else being equal, a longer lasting pleasure is better than one short-lived, whereas a short-lived pain is better than one lasting longer.

» *Certainty*. All else being equal, the more likely a pleasure will occur, the better, and the less likely a pain will occur, the better.

» *Propinquity*. All else being equal, the nearer a pleasure is in space or time, the better, and the more remote in space or time a pain is, the better. (It often makes more sense, for example, to "act local," helping someone close by rather than on the other side of the world.)

» *Fecundity*. All else being equal, the more a pleasure tends to produce more future pleasure, the better, the less a pain tends to produce more future pain, the better. (For example, the pleasure of physical exertion can help reinforce the habit and pleasure of regular exercise.)

» *Purity*. All else being equal, the less a pleasure tends to produce future pain, the better, and the more a pain tends to produce future pleasure, the better. (For example, the discomfort of taking a bitter-tasting medicine is usually worth it as a means to restoring health.)

» *Extent*. All else being equal, the greater the number of people experiencing pleasure, the better, the fewer the number experiencing pain, the better.

» *Kind*. All else being equal, a higher pleasure is better than a lower one, a higher pain—note the lack of inversion here—better than a lower one. (Think of pleasures and pains unique to human beings, such as the ability to enjoy culture or experience existential angst.)

The distinction between higher and lower pleasures requires some explanation and justification. Bentham's measures are quantitative, whereas Mill's is qualitative. Thus in leisure, for instance, we may consider one pleasure, say that of listening to classical music, to be better than that of listening to more popular music, even if the pleasures otherwise, that is quantitatively, count equivalently. This notion, in a leisure context, is already familiar to us, with contemplation counting for Aristotle as the highest form of leisure. Higher pleasures, for Mill, are similarly those appropriate for humans to experience uniquely: "It is better to be a human being dissatisfied than a pig satisfied; better to be Socrates dissatisfied than a fool satisfied" (*Utilitarianism* 2.6). To judge such matters, furthermore, one should have experience with both types of pleasure:

> If one of the two is, by those who are competently acquainted with both, placed so far above the other that they prefer it, even though knowing it to be attended with a greater amount of discontent, and would not resign it for any quantity of the other pleasure which their nature is capable of, we are justified in ascribing to the preferred enjoyment a superiority in quality so far outweighing quantity as to render it, in comparison, of small account. (*Utilitarianism* 2.5)

If those in a position to know agree, then the preferred pleasure is truly higher. If they fail to agree, or if they have no preference between the two, then neither ranks as superior.

If one is morally required to maximize utility, then it seems specific leisure activities, even leisure itself, will be justified to the extent, and only to the extent, that they do so. This apparent implication is particularly demanding. Perhaps leisure is never justified insofar as one could *always* make better use of one's time by doing more work or by being more active and productive rather than passive and relaxed. With Aristotle's virtue ethics, by contrast, there is no such problem, for leisure and particularly the best leisure express and fulfill the distinctive purpose of human beings irrespective of broader consequences. On a utilitarian view, however, leisure appears either incompatible with the moral demand to maximize utility or else instrumentally reducible to mere recreation, in recognition of the fact that sometimes we need rejuvenation for work. But even if utilitarianism is not too demanding of our leisure time or energy, it certainly seems to demand that we choose *better* rather than worse, but potentially *preferable*, forms of leisure, that we avoid, say, vegging out or enjoying mindless entertainment and instead opt for more mindful, intellectually engaging, morally edifying pursuits, high art instead of popular culture, in essence doing what we supposedly ought to do instead of what we would prefer to do. Not only does this seem to run counter to the point and spirit of leisure, it opens the door to snobbery, presumptuousness, and a worse problem even yet.

THE SPECTRE OF PATERNALISM

Although utilitarianism does provide some justification for leisure, or at least certain kinds of leisure, as a means of pleasure promotion, it also, paradoxically, gives rise to the spectre of paternalism. The word "paternalism," deriving from the Latin for father (*pater*), means telling someone what they can and can't do, or more mildly what they should and shouldn't do, in this respect treating them as a parent treats a child. In a leisure context this seems especially problematic, since life beyond leisure may strictly curtail or preclude, in the case of work or other obligations, what one wants to do. There are of course various laws against criminal behaviour irrespective of being at leisure, and even where one has a right to certain freedoms, such as freedom of speech, these rights are not absolute. Just as one may not steal a car and go on a joyride, so too it is common knowledge that one may not gratuitously yell "Fire!" in a crowded theatre as a prank or engage in hate speech. But restrictions on such behaviour, psychologically aberrant in a leisure context, represent only part of the issue.

Focusing specifically on leisure, Charles broaches the problem of paternalism as interfering with leisure: "[i]ntervention in the cycle of choice between leisure pleasures may take the form of persuasion or coercion through words and deeds.... Coercion may take the form of plans, rules, and regulations that must be obeyed by people at leisure" (52). Charles also lists various examples of such coercive laws and other regulations governing people's leisure choices (52–53): those governing certain forms of gambling, drug use, and sexual conduct; eligibility criteria for sports and other recreational activities; the requiring of safety gear such as helmets for cycling and other outdoor pursuits, lifejackets for boating, protective equipment for combat sports and martial arts, and so on. In many of these cases, whatever restrictions are in effect are meant to protect the health and safety of would-be participants. In some cases it seems that such paternalistic interference is appropriate, but in others it seems excessive, a sanctimonious and presumptuous kind of moralism. For instance, although there is ongoing controversy about whether to ban performance-enhancing drugs in sports, the virtual consensus is that children should not dope. Nor does anyone complain about action film stars or others taking such drugs as "image enhancers." As I put it elsewhere, "[t]here are no steroid bans in the film industry" (Holt, "Philosopher's Stallone" 66).

As much as Mill's utilitarianism seems to justify paternalistic restrictions on leisure, it often leads to a position that overreaches its proper scope. As expressed in, among other works, Mill's *On Liberty*, in the classic liberal view of society individual liberty is paramount and may only be legitimately restricted to prevent harm to other people (4.2). I may choose an unhealthy leisure practice such as getting drunk, and so long as I don't expose others to harm by, say, drinking and driving, to take one example, I am and should be free to do so. The implicit assumption here is that I can make a free, informed, rational choice. (In the case of intoxication or addiction, one's judgement, and ability to make rational choices for oneself, are acutely or chronically compromised. Getting drunk, then, involves choices that are progressively less and less autonomous.) Intuitively, and in legal terms, to a certain extent this is mapped by achieving the age of consent, typically eighteen years of age, though certain rules will be more or less age restrictive. Parents and guardians are charged with looking after the health and safety of children, whereas adults are left to provide for their own welfare, if they want to. As applied to adult leisure, many of the above restrictions remain in force irrespective of a subject's preferences.

One helpful way to understand the notion that some people are able to make certain decisions for themselves in leisure or in general, while others are not so able, is with the distinction between soft and hard paternalism. Both soft and hard paternalism impose restrictions on people's liberty in leisure and in general, but the presumed justification differs in the two cases. Starting with soft paternalism, a restriction may be imposed on subjects for their sake because they are unable to decide for themselves. Children are the paradigm case but by no means the only case here. Unlike adults, children are typically not allowed to stay up as late as they want, enjoy certain forms of entertainment, engage in dangerous sports, or explore other risky leisure pursuits, as adults do. Likewise, we sometimes restrict the freedom of adults with cognitive impairments, chronic or temporary, since they are like children in being unable to make free, rational decisions for themselves. In such cases, we are acting on others' behalf to ensure their health and safety. We may exclude children from skydiving or full-contact martial arts, for instance, though adults are typically allowed to pursue such activities.

In contrast to soft paternalism, a limit on liberty counts as hard paternalism when it is imposed on an individual or group even if they can make free, rational choices to decide for themselves. Here the justification is not to prevent harm to the subject but to prevent harm to others or society at large. As an extreme case, take murder, for which there are significant moral and legal penalties. In a leisure context we may consider the hypothetical case of recreational murder, which might make your skin crawl unless you are a fan of serial killer fiction or Alfred Hitchcock films. In the case of banning certain types of drug use, such as performance-enhancing drugs, or the campaign to ban combat sports like boxing and mixed martial arts, issues of presumed rational choice and informed consent seem to be marginalized in favour of protecting the health and safety of athletes. In the case of adult athletes specifically, there appears to be a presumption of compromised autonomy—by coercion, addiction, or obsession—such that we treat them as if they are children.

Turning from society at large to leisure professionals specifically, think of them as those whose expertise makes them not only well suited to being leisure educators and facilitators, but also, relatedly, better judges of the distinction between higher and lower pleasures available in general or in a certain realm of leisure experience (Charles 49). In considering how "intrusive" a leisure professional should be in people's leisure, Charles identifies a tightrope they need to walk between "authoritarian paternalism and laissez-faire anarchism" (51), that is, navigating a middle ground between just telling people what to do and letting them do whatever they want. Doing so means providing information about, exposure to, and opportunities for, worthier leisure activities, empowering people to make, as leisure-goers, wiser decisions about their own leisure, "to create autonomous individuals through respecting their liberty" in the leisure context (Charles 53). The best leisure educators make themselves dispensable, teaching their students to leave them behind in the development of their own expertise to judge for themselves which pleasures are worthy, in leisure and otherwise.

THE GOOD OF LEISURE

As we already know, leisure offers a multitude of goods: freeing us from work, the restorative value of recreation, enhancing social bonds through shared experiences, even cultural advancement when, say, an artist or intellectual devotes their leisure to personal passions the results of which become important to society at large. Such goods, among many others, however, do not account for *the good of leisure as leisure*—the essential good of intrinsically motivated elective activities—but only for the good of certain activities themselves, which could well not be intrinsically motivated or freely chosen. According to Wes Cooper, we need a positive theory of what the good of leisure is, as leisure ("Good of Leisure" 223). This will help strengthen the conceptual link between leisure and freedom: leisure not as freedom *from*, but as freedom *for*. This will require us to retrace an extended path along six different distinctions drawn by Cooper to generate six linked hypotheses, beginning with the general concept of good and ending with the specific good attaching to leisure itself rather than to the activities that alternately may or may not be leisure. This will improve our understanding of just how free we are, and ought to be, in leisure. We should note that the contrasts presented here are not meant to be dichotomies. Often a leisure choice will lie somewhere on the spectrum between the two extremes. Keep in mind that, for Cooper, leisure will be good, as leisure, insofar as it tends toward one extreme rather than the other.

» *Subject-neutral vs. subject-relative.* A goal is subject-neutral when the subject's leisure behaviour is good in a sense irrespective of whether it is good for the person themselves. Certain types of overspending of time or money on luxury items or gifts may be good for other people and for the economy, but not necessarily for the shoppers themselves. Cooper considers such economic goods to be subject-neutral, the kinds of good that a leisure theorist might be interested in, and approve of, from a social perspective, even if they have no effect or a detrimental effect on the leisure-goer themselves ("Good of Leisure" 224). The good of leisure, however, is not just good in some sense, or for someone, but for the subjects themselves.

» *Value-based vs. preference-based.* A good is value-based when it is objective, that is, transcends individual preferences, whereas it will be preference-based when it expresses a person's wishes no matter the objective value of what is preferred. Cooper's example is a debilitating leisure choice ("Good of Leisure" 224–25). Another example, as discussed earlier, is preferring a piece of popular entertainment to a work of fine art. Even if one has been sufficiently informed about objective values and higher pleasures, one may still sometimes or often prefer something else, and the good of leisure as leisure is preferential in precisely this sense.

» *Past/future-focused vs. present-focused.* To say that a good is future- or past-focused means it is motivated by considerations of the past or future rather than the present, as if one were living in the past or for tomorrow rather than in the moment. Holding oneself to past leisure practices or nostalgia is past-focused, whereas choosing a leisure activity for the sake of its results is more future-focused. Cooper identifies living for the sake of having no regrets as past-focused ("Good of Leisure" 225–26), but it seems more complex than that. Living so as to have no regrets (i.e., in the future) is clearly future-focused on what will *become* past-focused, namely the present. The "no regrets" principle might, after all, be a useful device for becoming more mindfully present in leisure.

As you might expect, the good of leisure as such is neither past- nor future-focused but present-focused instead.

- *Ill-considered vs. well-considered.* Cooper uses the technical term "cognitively suffused" instead of "well-considered," which is clearer but less precise. A person's leisure behaviour is cognitively suffused only "if it is what one would want to do if one were fully informed and thinking clearly" ("Good of Leisure" 226). If I make a rash and regrettable leisure choice after a few, or a few too many, drinks, my decision lacks cognitive suffusion in that my judgement is impaired such that I would choose otherwise if I were thinking clearly and not ignoring certain information or other personal preferences. The good of leisure here requires not just a vague sense that one would make the same choice in ideal circumstances, but that one really would do so.

- *Other-directed vs. self-directed.* A good is other-directed when its primary focus is one or more people other than oneself, self-directed when its primary focus is personal rather than altruistic. Some leisure might be equally concerned with self and other—sex, for instance—and morality is generally other-inclusive rather than purely or unreflectively selfish. For Cooper, however, there is something odd, even paradoxical, about a leisure that is purely concerned with others ("Good of Leisure" 225). Even if one finds altruism fulfilling—recall Telfer's leisure altruist in Chapter 3—it embodies the good of morality as morality rather than the good of leisure as leisure. The latter is, if perhaps inclusively, a self-concerned good.

- *Means-oriented vs. end-oriented.* The good of an activity is means-oriented when it derives from something extrinsic rather than intrinsic to the activity, though the latter is end-oriented. Recall the definition of leisure as intrinsically motivated elective activities. Take jogging. If one jogs not because one likes to but because of its health benefits, it is means-oriented and unleisurely. But, if one jogs because one enjoys it, it is to that extent leisurely. If both motivations are in effect, as presumably happens often, then the manifold goal of the activity will broadly include, but not be limited to, the end-oriented good of leisure.

Other Goods	The Good of Leisure
Subject-neutral	Subject-relative
Value-based	Preference-based
Past/future-focused	Present-focused
Ill-considered	Well-considered
Other-directed	Self-directed
Means-oriented	End-oriented

TABLE 8.1 *The good of leisure*

We may consider, though Cooper does not here, whether leisure activities that have additional, non-leisurely benefits are better, all else being equal, than leisure lacking such benefits. The answer may seem obvious, but it is not. As Cooper addresses elsewhere, in comparison with Plato, who thought that such extrinsic benefits could be aggregative, making leisure better, Aristotle, as we saw earlier, thought that they would result in a less pure form of leisure ("Leisure Theory" 6). Similarly, it is a quirk of human psychology that attaching extrinsic benefits to an activity is not necessarily aggregative and can diminish its intrinsic rewards (Holt and Pitter 22). For instance, an elite athlete could get caught up in money and fame and lose their love of the game.

To justify his nested hypotheses about the good of leisure, Cooper points to several theoretical benefits ("Good of Leisure" 227–28). First, because good leisure is often active, essentially end-oriented, and a positive good rather than the negative good of freedom from something undesirable, this account respects the important distinctions between freedom and idleness on the one hand and between leisure and recreation on the other. Second, the account also helps explain the incoherence of enforced leisure. Since good leisure is personally rewarding, one can't be forced either to be at leisure or engage in select forms of leisure without compromising their standing as leisure. Note the clear implications for colonial prescriptions of leisure deemed "appropriate" for Indigenous people. Lastly, the account fits traditional leisure theory, tracing back to Aristotle, about what work and life are for: we work for leisure's sake, and in a life so structured we find opportunities for real meaning and true fulfillment.

CONCLUSION

As broached earlier, the preceding discussion, from a non-Western perspective, may seem to reflect an overemphasis in Western culture on individual freedom in leisure and elsewhere. A colonial context in a sense complicates but also clarifies this picture. For instance, we might think, rightly, that an Indigenous Canadian should be free to choose among various leisure opportunities, whether a settler culture game like hockey or an Indigenous game like lacrosse, with the latter played either as appropriated by settler culture or as interpreted within traditional Indigenous culture. It may be more important, however, for Indigenous communities to prioritize solidarity, even in leisure, over individual freedom. Here, the locus of leisure's intrinsic motivation and elective status shifts, if only partly, from each community member to the community as a whole, though individual freedom, thus constrained, no doubt remains and remains essential to personal wellbeing.

QUESTIONS FOR CONSIDERATION

- What is the best way to address the tension between Mill's utilitarianism and his commitment to liberty?
- Are there any laws that restrict leisure or freedom generally that you think should be removed, relaxed, or introduced?
- Do you feel qualified to advise others about their leisure activities? Why or why not? At what point would you be overstepping your bounds?
- Does Cooper conflate the leisure/good leisure distinction?
- What, if anything, is wrong with taking a leisure theorist's perspective (subject-neutral or value-based) on leisure?
- What, if anything, is wrong with a leisure expert or professional prescribing or enforcing certain leisure activities?

© Austin Schmid Unsplash

CHAPTER 9

Leisure as Idleness

The more passive side of leisure is idleness, and the term has sometimes been used as a rough synonym for leisure itself. Here we treat leisure as a kind of idleness and idleness as a kind of leisure. According to thinkers like Bertrand Russell, leisure is what allows us to pursue worthy, culturally important if in some sense "useless" cultural pursuits, and so its value is chiefly to be found in such activities as distinct from various kinds of work focused on practical ends. Other theorists, however, see idleness in the more literal sense of leisure, in contrast to work, as more passive and decidedly unproductive either in a practical or a cultural sense of value. Idleness as leisure's more passive, less productive mode is presented as a worthy counterpart to its more active and productive modes.

INTRODUCTION

All along we have been talking about leisure in terms of elective activities, as things we choose to do. Even with Aristotle's rather passive notion of contemplative leisure, thinking about truth is still doing *something*, even if from an external standpoint it may seem as if the contemplator is doing nothing at all. Although contemplating truth or beauty is certainly on the more passive rather than active side of leisure from a physical point of view, it is not a lack of activity but rather a type of activity that is inner and psychological, the presence of which may have only subtle if any outward manifestations.

Still, the emphasis on leisure as intrinsically motivated elective *activities* seems to marginalize the equally if not more important passive side of leisure, that is, leisure as idleness. Indeed, we tend to associate activity with work and productivity, however fun, and in leisure we may allow ourselves to be idle instead of active. In terms of a work ethic, as we saw earlier, idleness often presents as a vice rather a virtue. Hence philosopher Bertrand Russell's provocative essay titled "In Praise of Idleness." We should note, however, that idleness itself, though negatively conceived as a lack of activity in some sense, also counts as an activity in its own right: idling. "Just idling" or "Nothing much" are perfectly good answers to the question "What are you doing?" Idleness requires us to discern another layer of interpretation in our definition of leisure. When I decide to do nothing in leisure, to laze on the sofa, daydream, or take a nap, for instance, this still counts as an activity, as doing something—lazing, daydreaming, or napping—and so fits our definition.

Before we begin, there is a further sense in which we can identify leisure, even vigorous active leisure, as idleness, and that is relative to work, which is remunerative, and other sorts of productivity deemed worthy by others. They may judge such pursuits to be *idle*, as wastes of time, energy, money, potential, and whatever other resources we may devote to them. In a crucial sense, then, idleness so-called may allow us to *opt out* of what other people think we should be doing, in the moment or long term, with our lives. This negative sense of idleness as freedom from others' expectations importantly complements and grounds the possibility of idleness as a freedom to pursue in leisure, irrespective of others' judgement, whatever we want, provided of course we do no harm to them in the process.

"IN PRAISE OF IDLENESS"

Russell begins his defence of idleness with the now-familiar contrast between a work ethic and a leisure ethic. Leisure here is understood as idleness, where idleness is distinguished from the drudgeries prized by a work ethic. When writing this piece in the early 1930s, Russell was concerned with what he saw as a widespread problem of too much work. In his words, "the road to happiness and prosperity [!] lies in an organized diminution of work" (B. Russell 3). As we have observed, many people even today suffer from overwork of various kinds and an excessive work ethic. The solution, for Russell, is to lessen the work of those who work too hard to the point where their labour is no longer excessive. We should have no more than a proper *amount* of unsatisfying work. In the extreme, Russell expresses the hope that leaders will teach young people "to do nothing" (2). Russell is working here, as we shall see, with an odd, somewhat ironic understanding of leisure, idleness, and work.

Much of the oddity in Russell's view, or more accurately in his expression of it, can be traced to his definition of work, which he gives explicitly by differentiating two levels and adding a supplemental third. Work means either "altering the position of matter at or near the earth's surface" or else "telling other people to do so" (B. Russell 3). Note that there is no mention in the definition itself of getting paid for such functions or any other reference to motive. What Russell does say about the psychology of each type is that "[t]he first type of work is unpleasant and ill paid; the second is pleasant and highly paid" (3). The supplemental third type, which for Russell is an extension of the second type, is that of people who advise those who give the orders about what orders to give and how to give them. As abstract as all this is, think of the first type as *manual* labour, the second type as *managerial*, and the third type as *advisory*. It will further help to illustrate with a concrete example such as construction work. Manual labour, skilled or unskilled, is work of the first type, moving matter around. We might think of the foreperson as doing managerial work, directing and overseeing the manual labour, and architects and engineers as advisors to those who commission the project. The foreperson, then, is a kind of go-between, giving specific orders for the implementation of plans approved from higher up.

Russell's view of work, and consequently of leisure and idleness, is deeply rooted in a historical perspective on the central importance of work prior to the Industrial Revolution, and how he thinks this should have changed but failed to in the wake of industrialization. Before the advent of industrialization, people could often produce through hard work little more than could meet their own and their families' basic needs, while any "small surplus above bare necessaries was not left to those who produced it, but was appropriated by warriors and priests" (B. Russell 4), either by force in the first case or persuasion, or some combination of the two, in the second. If one accepts that being generous and providing for others is a virtue, then one will readily so provide, even to those who would otherwise plunder. Sometimes, of course, providing for others is justified, as in the case of one's family and friends, and to a lesser extent one's community. However, as we have also seen, such a work ethic can be unnecessary and sometimes harmful, even abusive.

As Russell sums up, "[t]he morality of work is the morality of slaves, and the modern world has no need of slavery" (5). This is because, since the Industrial Revolution, we have a significantly reduced need to work hard to sustain ourselves compared with pre-industrial societies. Modernization has led to much greater leisure potential but not necessarily more, and in some cases far less, actual leisure than would be commensurate with that potential. Russell illustrates this with a hypothetical example of an innovation in manufacturing pins (6–7). Suppose someone devised a means of manufacturing pins twice as efficient as current methods. Assuming the number of pins produced is adequate to our needs, the rational thing to do would be to reduce the workday from, say, eight hours to four hours. However, this leisure potential is invariably spoiled. Innovation frees workers up not for more leisure but for more work, producing more pins than are necessary or, more intelligently if not more wisely, some other sellable product. Instead of a just work/leisure division *for* everybody, such as envisioned by Dewey, for instance, we have an unjust work/leisure division balancing out *across* individuals, with some having to work too hard to make up for those who don't work hard enough.

To clarify Russell's notion that an extreme work ethic represents a slave or slave state morality, consider another historically-minded account of how values change, Friedrich Nietzsche's (1844–1900) distinction between master and slave morality (*Genealogy* 7). In ancient times, the eras of Aristotle in Greece and Seneca in Rome, values were seen in terms of the virtues of the nobility, that is, those who were distinguished by their excellence, whether the courage of a great warrior-king or the wisdom of a great philosopher. Vice, as the opposite of virtue, was seen as the lack of such distinction, the province of the common, the masses. That was master morality. In many ways, however, in medieval and modern times a different kind of value system emerged and largely superseded master morality: slave morality, which *inverts* master morality, identifying the good not with the excellent but the common, and evil with what would distinguish itself from the common. For Nietzsche, this inversion was expressed in and realized by the rise of monotheistic religions, particularly Christianity, though modern thinkers may see various forms of atheistic collectivism in the same light.

In one respect, Russell's view of the value of leisure reflects Aristotle's theory, though in another it departs significantly and perhaps surprisingly. What Russell and Aristotle share is a commitment to the value of leisure as grounded in the human intellect in its proper sphere. For Aristotle, recall, the value of leisure is intrinsic, culminating in the contemplation of worthy things. For Russell, however, the value of leisure lies not in what it *is* but in what it *does*. It is not in the contemplation of truth and beauty that we find the value of leisure but in the active pursuit and creation of culturally valuable things: doing science, writing books, making art, and so on. For Russell, it is civilization that has intrinsic value and not—or not necessarily—leisure, which has a value largely reducible to advancing civilization. Thus Aristotle's model is a more plausible view of leisure as idleness, whereas Russell's model identifies leisure as idleness only with respect to the drudgeries of manual labour and the pleasures of its oversight. The structural injustice of past societies, formerly necessary to free the fortunate few for productive leisure, has become, in the wake of modernization, entirely dispensable.

SORTING OUT RUSSELL'S VIEW

To be clear, then, Russell is an advocate of "idleness" not per se but as a kind of productive leisure in the generation of culturally valuable if essentially "useless" things such as philosophy and art (Mumford 11). Idle hands, for Russell, are not the devil's workshop, but the culture's studio. What he praises is idleness as leisure and leisure as cultural achievement. Indeed, much of what Russell says about work and leisure stands at odds with most of what we have been saying in this book about both. By way of clarifying and critiquing Russell's view, we will now explore this tension.

Aside from the deliberate oddity of its formulation, we might take issue with Russell's definition of work and corresponding account of leisure in part by noting counterintuitive inclusions and exclusions from these categories. Mumford attributes this to what he calls Russell's "aristocratic account of human activities" (11), Russell notably being an aristocrat himself (his title was Earl). Take the work of university professors, for instance. There might be an elastic sense in which professors move matter (e.g., typing), or regulate its movement (e.g., during lecture), but this is not the sense of manual or managerial labour intended by Russell. Although some professors may qualify as doing advisory work in Russell's sense, as with professors of politics or the applied sciences, many in the liberal arts would not. Likewise, if moving matter is, as Russell contends, sufficient for the activity to count as work, this will fail to distinguish, say, the job of a bike courier from the activity of a recreational cyclist. Both would count as work for Russell irrespective of motive or context. In what follows we will pursue different strands of this theme.

Russell's assumed equivalence between physical exertion and manual work, where the latter is predominantly unpleasant and unintelligent, is, to say the least, oversimplified, not to mention the idea that such work is always bad (Mumford 18). An appropriate amount of physical exertion, whether what we would call manual labour or otherwise, is good for people, fostering their health and wellbeing against the inevitable pitfalls of a sedentary lifestyle. If we focus on the intrinsic value of enjoying a good mood, the fact that physical effort, paid or otherwise, can elevate one's mood is something Russell apparently fails to consider. Indeed, many people choose to include physical exertion in their leisure activities on a regular basis for precisely such reasons, among others. Not only is physical activity of certain kinds often quite pleasant, contra Russell, depending on the subject's preferences, of course, it can also be an outlet for intelligence, albeit practical. Garage tinkerers may come up with engineering fixes, and sportspeople may come up with play strategies useful within and in some cases beyond sport itself.

Notice that Russell's notion of the value of leisure as extrinsic, as useful in advancing civilization, runs afoul of our definition of leisure as elective activities that are intrinsically motivated. It is for Russell civilization rather than leisure that is intrinsically valuable, "useless" in a good way, the way Wilde had in mind, recall, when he claimed the same for art. Recall also from Chapter 3 the warnings from Dewey and other pragmatists to get away from the idea that practical use is mindless and intelligence impractical. It is no small irony that Russell's leisure ethic of advancing society turns out to be a kind of work ethic after all, because valuable leisure is that which produces theories and books and works of art. The best leisure for Russell turns out to be ... work!—only work of an intellectual kind that he would not identify as such. This view marginalizes the obvious fact that culture, even of the worthiest sort, involves both active and passive elements, production and consumption. In the culture of theatre, for instance, theatregoers are no less important than theatre-makers. It is on this decidedly more passive, non-remunerative side of the distinction that we find a much better claim to leisure, especially leisure as idleness. Relatedly, Russell's view also glosses over the possible neutral or negative effects of cultural production. A writer probably will be blind to whether their work, as they produce it, will affect the culture at all, much less the quality of that effect. Russell's own *Principia Mathematica* adds to the culture, but Hitler's *Mein Kampf* detracts from it—significantly.

Consider again the question of whether my writing this book is or is not leisure. The answer is not obvious. It is an enjoyable and worthwhile process, but it also advances my career and contributes in some small way to the culture. As a professor, I am expected to do research, to produce such work, but I get to choose which projects to pursue, and how, and at what pace to pursue them. Since I have tenure and full professorship, moreover, I do not strictly have to undertake such major projects at all anymore. Nor will the little money I get in royalties make this book worth my while financially. Is it intrinsically motivated? Well, partly. Is it elective? Well, kind of. The great irony is that Russell wrote "In Praise of Idleness" and *hundreds* of other popular essays and books—for the money, because he needed the money (Mumford 5). Although Russell would describe such writing as idleness, as paid and necessary leisure, it seems far more plausible to describe the production of such works as work, albeit intellectual work unconnected to the oversight of manual work per se.[1] Useful things may be worthy, and worthy things useful.

To diagnose the problem here, though there may be more than one, it seems to lie in Russell's objective descriptions of work and leisure activities apart from the agent's motives and circumstances. The notion of work as connected with moving matter suggests that Russell was partly, if unconsciously, inspired by physics, where work is defined as a force causing the displacement of an object. But because leisure requires intrinsic motivation and elective status, these elements of a subject's psychology are not captured by a characterization of work as either consisting in or connected with manual effort. Someone moving matter around may be working for a paycheque and hating the process of, say, lugging construction materials. Someone else may be moving matter as a recreational or leisure activity, and loving it, as with a bodybuilder lifting weights. Someone directing such activity, likewise, could be either a foreperson or a coach, and either could, at least in principle, either be professionalized or leisurized, depending again on the subject's motivation and ability to choose.

RECENT APPROACHES, IDLE CONCERNS

Whereas Russell construes idleness rather peculiarly as a kind of active productivity, cultural rather than material, more recent approaches to idleness construe it more conventionally as less strenuous and less productive. Trainer, for example, construes idleness in terms of what is usually a minimal description, if not an adequate definition, of leisure as "non-productive consumption of time" (116). In a similar vein, Gini champions the crucial role of being disposed to idleness, especially vacationing, in a culture of overwork

1 One could argue, however, that in proposing a four-hour workday, for instance, Russell's "In Praise of Idleness" counts as advisory work in his sense.

such as ours, in his book *The Importance of Being Lazy*. Likewise, in an analysis drawing on select sources in the history of thought, O'Connor advocates idleness in a decidedly passive and unproductive sense, as our best and perhaps only means of being truly free from the norms and expectations governing the rest of our lives, whether at work or at leisure. Idleness, on this view, is our escape to true freedom from goal-directed, structured activity, on the clock or off, and however enjoyable.

For O'Connor, more specifically, idleness frees us from presumptive obligations to be active and productive irrespective of, and across, the work/leisure distinction. The back cover of O'Connor's book announces providing "[t]he case for idleness as freedom from usefulness, performance, and the opinion of others" and arguing "that the case against an indifference to work and effort is flawed—and that idle aimlessness may instead allow for the highest form of freedom." Idleness is not work, or productivity, or in any appreciable way activity. We already distinguish idleness from leisure in some sense, since leisure may be active, even productive, where idleness is neither. But O'Connor goes further:

> For most who enjoy it, leisure is an instrument, allowing us to cede temporarily from life-shaping demands. Yet it is implicated in those demands. Leisure can renew our capacity to perform. It allows us to recover from labor or to think freely about our next task or to augment ourselves by taking the trouble to gain valuable new experiences (cultural tourism and the like). In today's world, leisure may be considered a liberation of a sort, yet many labor regimes make leisure—paid vacation leave—obligatory. Leisure is good, apparently, not only for the worker but also for the employer. (7–8)

In O'Connor's view, then, leisure fits a work-centred view of living in a way that idleness does not. Thus it is idleness, not leisure, that allows "liberation from tasks and pressures. And idleness appears to be valued because it is the actual experience of that liberation" (173). Idleness, on this view, is true freedom from all productive activity, not a false freedom to pursue other, more rewarding types of productive activity. That, in a nutshell, is O'Connor's view.

Taking a cue from O'Connor, J.S. Russell (not to be confused with Bertrand) also praises idleness as an important part of a good life, although by itself probably not sufficing for a sufficiently meaningful one. For Russell, though, idleness is not best thought of as implicitly unproductive and inactive along the lines proposed by O'Connor. Rather, it is best conceived in terms of play and leisure, or better as certain varieties of play and leisure ("Play and Leisure" 304). To give us a better sense of what he means, Russell offers various intuitive and helpful examples:

> enjoying an unhurried coffee and a pleasurable read or a conversation over breakfast—or listening to music, hanging out with friends, pottering in the garden, noodling on a musical instrument, going on walkabouts, relaxing with a drink, watching TV, reading in bed, getting up slowly in the morning, taking in the autumn leaves or spring flowers, enjoying a long bath or shower, relaxing quietly at a friend's cottage.... ("Play and Leisure" 304–05)

What these examples make clear is that idleness is not necessarily a lack of activity or even productivity but rather a lack of strenuous activity and concerted efforts to get things done. To put the point another way, where O'Connor sees idleness as a state of being—inactive and unproductive—Russell sees it as a mode of being, a modifier. In grammatical terms, think adverb rather than noun or verb. Idleness here isn't a matter of doing nothing but of doing things in a leisurely manner—in which case "idly" and "leisurely" are close in meaning—unhurried, without straining body or mind. Most of Russell's examples are activities that may be done idly, as he describes, or otherwise.

There are two further points of criticism that complement Russell's. First, although I agree with O'Connor that we must be clear about the important distinction between idleness and leisure, I believe he errs in drawing that distinction. Whereas idleness does exclude the more active and productive forms of leisure that J.S. Russell and O'Connor would agree are not idle—except perhaps in Bertrand Russell's peculiar sense—O'Connor sees idleness as wholly distinct from rather than the less active or productive part of leisure overall. But if you revisit his description of leisure above, as an instrument, as escape from and restoration for work, as work-concerned and -defined, what he has in mind seems to be recreation rather than leisure, or else a misguided reduction of leisure to recreation. Recall that recreation is to be distinguished from leisure in precisely this way, in being valued instrumentally in fostering work, rather than intrinsically as an end in itself. This conflation is unfortunate and apparently unintentional.

The same applies to my second point of criticism, namely that O'Connor's account of idleness as an ideal implies a purely negative sense of freedom: freedom *from* rather than freedom *for* or freedom *to*. Recall that understanding leisure as freedom *from* is a thin and theoretically insufficient one, whereas leisure as freedom *for*, or *to* do, certain activities is more theoretically adequate. Similar considerations apply to idleness, which in O'Connor's sense supplants the role of leisure in an account of what allows us to be truly free (180). O'Connor insists that his is not a negative account of idleness, but his protest reinforces a negative interpretation: idleness "is misaligned with negative freedom. This is because it is not merely 'freedom from' but should be understood as a positively experienced freedom *from* specific constraints" (180; emphasis added). Indeed, O'Connor depicts positive freedom in the form of, say, play or leisure as often if not inevitably goal-directed and structured and so less than ideally free (180). Note that idleness itself can be usefully understood as both goal-directed (taking it easy, relaxing) and constrained (not too vigorous, not too productive), although this construal, however intuitive, is not necessarily decisive.

CONCLUSION

Let me be clear that despite the above critiques of Bertrand Russell's and O'Connor's strikingly different views of idleness, each gets something importantly right about leisure as idleness, even if, especially in the latter case, this way of framing their insights might not be welcome. Russell is right that it is not just inactivity but also activities deemed impractical that people often dismiss as a waste of time or leisure. O'Connor is right too that meaningful freedom means exemption not just from work but also from the goals and structures imposed, rightly or wrongly, by other people or society at large. Some people may prefer, or need, more idleness in leisure than others. We need idleness to the extent that we would otherwise be too active. But we can be too idle too, and that is also an extreme best avoided. The happy medium is a balance between the two kinds of leisure, assuming that work is not too demanding or not demanding enough. In such cases, significantly more or significantly less idleness may be ideal to achieve a proper balance. Leisure is not solely a corrective, of course, but can be inclusively so. This gives us more than a glimpse of the richly pluralistic nature of leisure as an inclusive source of meaning in our lives.

QUESTIONS FOR CONSIDERATION

- Can Russell's definition of work accommodate in any meaningful sense the work of intellectuals unconcerned with manual labour or its oversight?
- Although Russell seems to marginalize the intrinsic value of leisure itself, do you think he has a point about good leisure contributing to civilization?
- Given Russell's understanding of idleness as productive leisure, is there any room in his account for genuine idleness (i.e., passive and unproductive leisure)?
- Is idleness best understood as inactive and unproductive (à la O'Connor), as less active and less productive (à la J.S. Russell), or in both senses?
- Can O'Connor be defended from the charge of providing a largely negative view of idleness and freedom, and if so on what basis?
- What do you consider the ideal balance between active and idle leisure, or between productive and unproductive leisure?

© Nick Fewings/Unsplash

CHAPTER 10
Authenticity and Leisure

In terms of philosophical theories, the connection that we find in leisure between freedom and finding or creating meaning in life fits well with and is perhaps best expressed by existentialism. From an existential perspective, what matters most in leisure and life is being true to oneself, being authentic. What makes for authentic leisure is something that only individuals can decide for themselves. This view implies a thoroughly pluralistic approach to leisure, bringing together various strands of thought throughout this book. If leisure is important for creating meaningful lives for ourselves, we will question its ultimate value in that work likewise may—though often fails to—provide opportunities for creating meaning and achieving fulfillment. The role of leisure in a meaningful life, then, turns out to be contextual as well, depending on the degrees and kinds of fulfillment available elsewhere in one's life.

INTRODUCTION

We have already discussed in some detail freedom in connection with leisure and have also mentioned at various turns the importance of leisure for many people in creating meaning and fulfillment in life. We turn now to an influential approach to the question of meaning in life: existentialism, which designates a group of diverse but thematically unified philosophies and artworks beginning in the nineteenth century with thinkers like Søren Kierkegaard and Friedrich Nietzsche and achieving prominence in the twentieth century with philosophical literati like Jean-Paul Sartre, Simone de Beauvoir, and Albert Camus. Despite similar approaches to the question of meaning in life, existentialism encompasses different philosophical commitments and work in a wide array of high and popular artforms. Kierkegaard was a theist, whereas Sartre was an atheist, yet both are exponents of existentialism. Samuel Beckett's slow-moving, esoteric play *Waiting for Godot* (1953) stands toe-to-toe as existentialist art with William Friedkin's fast-paced, frenetic neo-noir film *To Live and Die in L.A.* (1985).

As a first step, think of existentialism as not just asserting the importance of human freedom but *radicalizing* it. That is, existentialists see freedom as much more extensive and profound than we usually take it to be. On reflection, our individual freedom is fundamental to our existence, an inevitable burden and a bracing opportunity. We can illustrate this, in part, with Sartre's well-known example of someone working as a waiter in a restaurant. For Sartre, someone in such a job should not see themselves *merely* as a waiter, whose actions are determined or made meaningful by that role (*Being* 82). As we have been discussing all along, work is something often described as necessary in contrast to leisure, where we find freedom. However, it is only hypothetically necessary. Sartre's waiter is no less free to go to work or not on a given day, to stay in that job or find another of the same or another kind. Even employment itself is not strictly necessary, even if one "needs" the money. One can always opt out, choosing unemployment, however undesirable that outcome may be. Freedom to choose among available options is more limited in work than in leisure, but it remains fundamentally present.

THE EXISTENTIALIST WORLDVIEW

Sketching the existentialist worldview in general will help motivate and explain how it bears particularly on leisure. At the risk of oversimplification, the existentialist worldview has two main facets: an account of the way the world *is*, specifically the situation of individual human beings in the world, as well as how we *ought* to regard and comport ourselves in that situation (Holt, "Existential Ethics" 51). The former is what we might call existentialist metaphysics, the latter existentialist ethics. We will look at each in turn.

The existentialist commitment to radical freedom has two aspects, the first concerning human nature, the second concerning objective prescriptions of value or action. Both sides are negative in the following sense. On the one hand, freedom means a denial of human nature as a determinant of what we essentially are or what we contingently do. This is not a denial of biological properties, of instincts or natural inclinations, and these do limit our possibilities for action and value, but they do not decide such matters for us. Hunger may incline me to eat a certain thing at a certain time, but I may choose either to eat something else or at a later time instead. On the other hand, freedom means denying any objective prescription for what to value or what to do. Sartre recounts the example of a student who asked advice about a dilemma: whether to fight for his country in the war or stay at home to care for his sick mother (*Existentialism* 30). In such a case, no one can decide from the outside which value should prevail, which project to pursue.[1] A person must decide for themselves.

Arising from the commitment to radical freedom is a corollary view of the meaning of life and what makes it worthwhile, a perspective with both a negative and a positive side. On the negative side, the existentialist will insist that meaning for an individual is *not* readymade. It is not received or handed down. It does not come from outside the subject. Nature does not give meaning to one's life, nor does culture, or morality, or a divine being, no matter one's beliefs about such beings. Nor does the meaning of one's life originate in other people, though it may involve them: family, friends, mentors, or partners. Just as others cannot in the final analysis determine our values or actions, so too they cannot decide for us what gives meaning to our choices, our actions, our projects, and our lives. On the positive side, each individual must create meaning for themselves. Leisure, as we know, gives each of us particularly fruitful opportunities to make meaningful choices and lives for ourselves. This situation, again, is both a burden and an opportunity.

Slogans like "You are what you do" and "You are the sum total of your choices" seem to capture the combination of radical freedom and self-made meaning that we find in existentialism. Sartre's rather enigmatic slogan is "Existence precedes essence" (*Existentialism* 20), which expresses the uniqueness of human beings in contrast to other living creatures, inanimate objects,

---

1 Different existentialists have different views of the limits of freedom here. Both of the student's choices comport with conventional morality, whereas Nietzsche's *Übermensch* is not constrained by conventional morality.

and artifacts. Think of automotive assembly lines or Ikea furniture, where things are built by design to certain specifications and for certain functions. Such objects are predetermined in purpose, action, and meaning, and such predetermination is by design, natural or human, or some combination of the two (indeed, human design is constrained by natural law). Unlike manufactured objects, which are *made*, human subjects are *thrown* into the world, not *pre*determined but *self*-determined in purpose, action, and meaning, not by divine or natural forces but by the subject's own choices and values. Human beings make their own unique essence out of the raw materials of their own unique existence.

In the face of such "thrownness," it may be hard to appreciate that an existentialist could have any moral commitments at all. Most existentialists, however, are committed to a form of moral stance that requires authenticity. This moral outlook, the existential imperative, can be expressed as "Be true to yourself" or "Be authentic" (Holt, "Existential Ethics" 52). Although this may appear to be the kind of objective prescription that existentialists reject, it does not presume to tell us *what* to do or value but *how* to coordinate our acts and our values, and how to think of oneself as the author of these acts and values for ourselves. Being authentic, being true to oneself, here implies acknowledging one's freely chosen values and actions, following through on them, as well as taking responsibility for such choices. If authenticity is *the* existential virtue par excellence, then the opposite, the existential vice, is inauthenticity or bad faith: blaming other people or circumstances for one's choices, acting contrary to one's values, any attempt to disburden oneself of radical freedom.

To further clarify what authenticity means in this context, think of it as a *formal* virtue, in other words not a matter of content, of what to choose or value, but a matter of form, of how to choose and value, and how to act given one's values. In this way authenticity is like other such virtues like integrity (acting in accordance with one's values, whatever they are) or honesty (saying what one believes to be true, whatever it is) (Holt, "Existential Ethics" 52). Thus the existentialist's sense of "authenticity" fits, to some extent, our commonsense notion of the word: an authentic person is a *genuine* person. Likewise, inauthenticity is a formal vice, a failure to be genuine, like hypocrisy (acting contrary to the values one espouses) or dishonesty (assertions contrary to one's beliefs, whatever they may be). But even though existentialist ethics appears to be a morality of pure form, it can require a real, more traditional virtue: courage (Holt, "Existential Ethics" 54). It is often a courageous act to stand up for one's commitments, especially in the face of resistance. Inauthenticity is often the result of cowardice or what philosophers call *akrasia*, or weakness of will. What all this means for leisure, or what leisure should be, we turn to next.

AUTHENTIC LEISURE

The implications of existentialism for the philosophy of leisure should be clear enough. Such a connection is made explicitly by Coe, who discusses "the place of leisure in our lives" as tied to not only "the good life" but also "what it means to be human" (91). This applies, of course, no less to the ancient Greeks than to modern existentialists. We might see existentialism, as Coe does, as the end of a historical progression in philosophizing about leisure from ancient to modern times. Leisure is a longstanding object of reflective concern, since it is an expression of freedom, unlike necessary work, yet a potential source of meaning, like certain forms of elective work. If the existentialist stance describes the human condition generally, then it applies across both work and leisure contexts. Work may not always be authentic, but leisure, as a more open field of possibilities available to subjects less constrained by logistics and necessity, can and should be authentic. Authenticity may therefore legitimately override other desirable kinds and qualities of leisure: active, creative, intellectual, or any leisure of any presumed higher type. For certain people in certain situations, a more passive, receptive, lower pleasure yielding leisure could prove more authentic than conforming to external expectations about the leisure one ought to pursue, even those forms that others might well consider more authentic.

Authentic leisure, as with authenticity generally, requires avoiding various pitfalls indicative of bad faith. For instance, if one treats oneself as an object rather than a subject in leisure, as something to be worked into shape through exercise, for instance, if one fails to recognize and embrace being free as a subject in such physical activity, then it will be inauthentic. One will likewise be inauthentic if one fails to take responsibility for one's leisure choices, if for instance one regrets spending all day playing videogames—not that one must regret this, or that playing such games cannot be authentic—and attributes this, say, to the fact that one had a hard week, or that one was going along with other people's desires: this amounts to an inauthentic choice. Again, authenticity often requires courage, both in leisure and in everyday life. It may also be both courageous and authentic to let others take the lead, whether leisure experts in own one's culture or guides to authentic leisure experiences in other cultures.

Because it is predicated on radical freedom, authenticity in leisure and in general is inconsistent with various forms of scientific and social determinism, the idea roughly that an individual's actions are decided not by them but by natural or social forces. The explanatory and technological power of science as a deterministic worldview is so impressive, in so many ways, that it seems hard to deny the apparent implication that human freedom is illusory. From a social perspective too we seem to be products of our surrounding culture, a culture that not only influences our choices but makes them for us (Carr 144). We saw this concern earlier reflected in Ramsay's argument against unreflective consumerist leisure. We do not really have a choice, or a meaningful one at any rate, to be presented with an array of products and services that are effectively superficial, frivolous, and the desire for which is artificially generated for the sake of predominantly shallow and cynical capitalist interests. Authenticity itself may be at best a hollow virtue and at worst delusional. Still, perhaps what matters most in considering the determinism question is not whether we are free in fact but whether we *believe* we are (Godbey 5). In the words of Simone de Beauvoir, "whatever the case may be, we believe in freedom" (23). Quality leisure will be earmarked by the subject's enhanced sense of freedom even if the feeling proves illusory.

Such an existentialist slant may be read into Blackshaw's notion of liquid leisure, where leisure is the context for "our human goal of satisfying our hunger for meaning and our thirst for giving our lives a purpose" (Blackshaw 120). On this metaphor, leisure is "dynamic and fluid" with an essence that "lies in the search for happiness, pleasure, and freedom" (Bouwer and van Leeuwen 587). Liquid leisure is very much existential leisure and involves "creating our own meaningful truths" within the context of "artful living" (Bouwer and van Leeuwen 595). To some extent this reflects Nietzsche's notion of authenticity as making one's life into a work of art (*Gay Science* 290, 299). Liquid leisure has not only an artistic but also a spiritual dimension, which is echoed in Carr's account of good or authentic leisure as a spiritual matter concerned with personal enlightenment (149). These parallels with authenticity are intuitive enough on some level. However, despite their suggestiveness and plausibility, they fall short of a wider—thicker, as it were—pluralism in what counts as good or authentic leisure. Living one's life artfully seems attractive, no doubt, but it also seems demanding. Artful living could be authentic leisure for some people some of the time, but not everyone needs or wants to live that way. Sometimes the authentic leisure choice will be neither spiritual nor artful.

THICK LEISURE PLURALISM

On some level we are probably all pluralists about leisure. The conviction that some leisure activities are better than others is perfectly compatible with the commitment to leisure as an inherently free domain manifesting in a range of different permissible activities to choose from and, within this scope, a range of laudable activities. In leisure, at least, if nowhere else, you can do what you want, and I can do what I want. One may be committed to sport, for instance, as a worthy leisure activity, and even work to make it accessible to everybody, without requiring that people play sports or, more absurdly, some presumed best sport. Some people prefer less active leisure, or a different kind of active leisure, and that's okay.

The notion that leisure preferences may vary across individuals is hard to deny and constitutes what I call *thin* leisure pluralism: different people have permissibly different leisure preferences. What I am advocating, however, is a more robust pluralism, a *thick* leisure pluralism. If we really do care about authenticity, which we should, then the freedom of leisure yields a range of live options running counter to many normative accounts of leisure that are in fact less pluralistic than they seem. Below I will sketch what I take to be the important elements of thick leisure pluralism, partly inspired and partly justified by the existentialist premium on authenticity.

1. An important and fairly uncontroversial feature of preferences is their tendency to change over time. As we mature, for instance, our tastes change, and this will inform our leisure preferences. A superficial and false reading of authenticity may enjoin us to remain true to our past selves or to some imagined future self. But such nostalgic or forward-looking attitudes are not necessarily authentic for us in the moment and may constitute bad faith. Being authentic means being true to ourselves in the present rather than holding ourselves to external standards—even our own past or presumed future standards. My current preferences may be reaffirmed in the future and provide both structure and integrity to my life, or they may change next month, tomorrow, or by the time I finish this sentence.

2. Another important element of thick leisure pluralism is that leisure-goers may have permissibly varied preferences not just over time but at any given time. Even if we ought to seek the higher pleasures in leisure, this doesn't mean we can't or shouldn't ever seek some of the lower ones as well. I may enjoy listening to popular music as well as to opera,

even if I believe the latter to be qualitatively better. My leisure needs and preferences may, and perhaps should, be variable in this way—a varied leisure diet, as it were. Different balances may likewise be more suited to, and more authentic for, different individuals. Some thrive on a greater preponderance of higher leisure, or lower, others still on a balance between the two.

3. A related facet of the thick pluralist position recognizes and respects that a person's work and other non-leisure contexts should inform their decisions about the kinds of leisure that would suit them best. For instance, views of leisure that prioritize activity over passivity, or vice versa, or creativity over appreciation, or vice versa, for *everyone* irrespective of an overall perspective on an individual's life, are unhelpfully monolithic. A person who has a physically demanding job, for instance, may resist the call to creative activity as not just inauthentic but also inappropriate for them. If one's profession is sedentary but gratifying on an intellectual or creative level, they may find more active—but not necessarily intellectual or creative—forms of leisure to be more authentic. One may need little or no active, creative, intellectual, or productive leisure if one is surfeited with such activities at work. By contrast, where some or all of these are insufficient at work, leisure can provide ample opportunities to answer such needs and preferences, provided one hasn't been overtaxed by work or other obligations—a big if.

4. Some of the variability covered so far has been framed in general terms, which is limited to the extent that leisure needs and preferences may vary across individuals having virtually the same life situation. Take meaning. Suppose A and B both find their jobs and other commitments to be to some degree meaningful but less than completely fulfilling. In this context, A may feel a deep need, an irresistible urge, to express themselves in an artistic medium, say poetry. On the other hand, B may find the same lack of complete fulfillment far less motivating, not a motivation for more passive leisure, perhaps, but a less pronounced need for fulfilling leisure at all. Writing the occasional poem could provide some pleasure for B, and that may suffice, even if it falls short of the essential validation A seeks in the same activity. Not everyone needs meaningful leisure.

5. This brings up the last and likely most controversial part of my proposed thick leisure pluralism, the idea that the importance of freedom

and even authenticity as we have discussed may vary across individuals and cultures alike. We have already encountered this notion in part in earlier chapters. People outside the Western tradition may see individual freedom in leisure as far less important than cultural solidarity in exercising freedom of the community. In Western culture, too, one may simply be less interested in helping to decide, say, what leisure activities a friend or family group will pursue. There may be moral and social concerns lurking here, questions of injustice concerning group dynamics where some adopt dominant and others submissive roles. But there is also a meta level at which these leisure preferences could also make sense in terms of individual freedom and authenticity. One can always opt out. I should be free in leisure not to consider my freedom in leisure all that important. It may be most authentic for me in leisure not to care much about being authentic in leisure.

DOES LEISURE MATTER?

The above sketch of thick leisure pluralism is certainly permissive and perhaps too much so, which gives the possible impression that leisure can legitimately mean just about anything to anyone, hollowing out the concept of leisure. This impression is understandable but misguided. Not just anything will count as leisure much less good or authentic leisure. Since leisure is, by definition, intrinsically motivated elective activities, anything that is not so motivated or so chosen won't properly count as leisure. Still, a nagging scepticism may remain. If what we seek and value in leisure is also available in work and other domains, to what extent, if any, is leisure itself important? At the end of the day, does leisure matter?

Think of this problem in terms of meaning and authenticity. If what we seek is a meaningful life authentically lived, then so long as we have such a life, it seems to matter little to us where its meaning comes from. A life made meaningful through one's work, if one must work, seems no less and in some ways more desirable than one made meaningful primarily through leisure, or one in which both sources of meaning are of similar importance. Indeed, some people are fortunate enough to have their work and leisure lives so well integrated that the difference between the two, while real, is of no importance, and may even be difficult to assess in certain cases. Consider again the case of me writing this book. Russell would consider it leisure rather than work, though it helps fulfill one of my work duties, doing research; yet despite the effort, which is substantial, I find it a lot of fun, and I do not strictly need to write a book to keep my job. So, is it work or leisure? Well, both, kind of.

For another case, a few years ago I became a practitioner of taekwondo, for fun and for fitness, but also to inform my ongoing work on martial arts and combat sports, and to complement a longstanding interest in martial arts cinema. As freely chosen, it is elective, but I can't disentangle what appears to be intrinsic motivation (fun, fulfillment) from what is clearly also instrumental motivation (informing my work). The true motivation seems to be integrating different aspects of my life in a way that blurs the distinction between intrinsic and instrumental reward. I simply cannot tell whether my motivation counts as sufficiently intrinsic to constitute leisure. But if such activities give meaning to my life, they apparently do so irrespective of qualifying as leisure. So again, does leisure matter?

To answer this question, I will now present a constructive dilemma in order to bring this book to a close. Consider first a life that is ideal, or close to ideal, at least with some degree of plausibility. Fill in the details as you like. One guiding theme throughout this book has been that, in essential terms, the value of work is instrumental whereas the value of leisure is intrinsic. From Aristotle to Suits, one works in unfulfilling ways, if one does, to survive and for the sake of leisure, which means one would rationally choose not to do such work if one did not have to. That is, one would abandon activities done merely for instrumental reasons to achieve ends more readily available otherwise. This isn't to say that utopian life would involve no effort whatsoever, even strenuous exertion, since these may be elements in preferred forms of play, games, and other leisure activities. In an ideal world, then, leisure would matter because life would *consist* in leisure, in gratuitous activities chosen for their own sake, because no other type of purpose would be on the table.

Life as we know it, however, is far from ideal. Most of us have to work for a living, and for many this time and energy consuming necessity yields less than a full measure of meaning and fulfillment even when leisure is factored in. Work may be good not only as facilitating leisure, but also, as we have seen, as a source of meaning and fulfillment. If everyone had highly rewarding jobs, that would itself be a kind of utopia, one perhaps barely distinguishable from a utopia of leisure. But since that is, for many people, far removed from the real world, leisure is valuable both as an end to which less-than-fulfilling work is a means, and as a counterweight to the unfortunate effects of such work in achieving a realistically if not perfectly balanced life.

Leisure therefore matters, either as the very stuff of an ideal life or as a reward and consolation for a life less than ideal. However little or great the distance between the ideal and our own lives, then, and whether we think of it as leisure or not, whether we even think of it at all, leisure matters.

QUESTIONS FOR CONSIDERATION

- To what extent does the existentialist outlook reflect your own thinking about life or leisure? Is there something important that existentialist views neglect or simply get wrong?
- Can you identify more and less authentic leisure choices you have made, and to what extent is being authentic in leisure important to you?
- What is the difference between being an authentic leisure-goer and having an authentic leisure experience?
- Do you agree with the thick leisure pluralism proposed above, or do you think it either goes too far or not far enough in embracing diversity in leisure?
- To what extent should diversity in leisure reflect sociocultural differences along with differences in individual taste?
- How important ultimately is leisure to you, and how important is it that your attitude reflect any objective assessment of leisure's true value?

Works Cited

Allen, Barry. "Games of Sport, Works of Art, and the Striking Beauty of Asian Martial Arts." *Journal of the Philosophy of Sport*, vol. 40, no. 2, 2013, pp. 241–54. https://doi.org/10.1080/00948705.2013.785418

Aristotle. *Nicomachean Ethics*. Translated by Leslie Brown, Oxford University Press, 2009.

Beardsley, Monroe C. "What Is Going on in a Dance?" *Dance Research Journal*, vol. 15, no. 1, pp. 31–36.

Bentham, Jeremy. "The Principle of Utility." *Introduction to Philosophy: Classical and Contemporary Readings*, 3rd ed., edited by John Perry and Michael Bratman, Oxford University Press, 1999, pp. 483–86.

Best, David. *Philosophy and Human Movement*. George Allen & Unwin, 1978.

Blackshaw, Tony. *Leisure*. Routledge, 2010.

Bouwer, Johan, and Marco van Leeuwen. "The Meaning of Liquid Leisure." *Routledge Handbook of Leisure Studies*, edited by Tony Blackshaw, Routledge, 2013, pp. 584–96.

Carr, Neil. "Rethinking the Relation Between Leisure and Freedom." *Annals of Leisure Research*, vol. 20, no. 2, 2017, pp. 137–51. https://doi.org/10.1080/11745398.2016.1206723

Charles, John M. "On Liberty and Leisure." *Leisure and Ethics: Reflections on the Philosophy of Leisure*, edited by Gerald S. Fain, American Alliance for Health, Physical Education, Recreation and Dance, 1991, pp. 47–57.

Chisholm, Roderick M. *The Problem of the Criterion*. Marquette University Press, 1973.

Coe, William. "Leisure, Transcendence, and the Good Life: From the Greeks to the Existentialists." *Leisure and Ethics: Reflections on the Philosophy of Leisure*, edited by Gerald S. Fain, American Alliance for Health, Physical Education, Recreation and Dance, 1991, pp. 91–99.

Confucius. *Analects*. Translated by Edward Slingerland, Hacket, 2003.

Cook, Doug. *Taekwondo: Ancient Wisdom for the Modern Warrior*. YMAA Publication Center, 2001.

Cooper, Wes. "Some Philosophical Aspects of Leisure Theory." *Leisure Studies: Prospects for the Twenty-First Century*, edited by Edgar L. Jackson and Thomas L. Burden, Venture, 1999, pp. 3–15.

——. "What Is the Good of Leisure?" *Leisure and Ethics: Reflections on the Philosophy of Leisure*, edited by Gerald S. Fain, American Alliance for Health, Physical Education, Recreation and Dance, 1991, pp. 223–29.

de Beauvoir, Simone. *The Ethics of Ambiguity*. Citadel Press, 1948.

de Grazia, Sebastian. *Of Time, Work, and Leisure*. Doubleday, 1962.

Dewey, John. *Democracy and Education*. Simon & Brown, 2012.

Forsyth, Janice, Christine O'Bonsawin, Russell Field, and Murray G. Phillips. "Ways of Knowing: Sport, Colonialism, and Decolonization." *Decolonizing Sport*, edited by Janice Forsyth, Christine O'Bonsawin, Russell Field, and Murray G. Phillips, Fernwood Publishing, 2023, pp. 1–20.

Fox, Karen. "Leisure and Indigenous Peoples." *Leisure Studies*, vol. 25, no. 4, 2006, pp. 403–09. https://doi.org/10.1080/02614360600896502

Gini, Al. *The Importance of Being Lazy: In Praise of Play, Leisure, and Vacation*. Routledge, 2003.

Godbey, Geoffrey. 2003. *Leisure in Your Life: An Exploration*. 6th ed., Venture, 2003.

Goodale, Thomas, and Geoffrey Godbey. *The Evolution of Leisure: Historical and Philosophical Perspectives*. Venture, 1988.

Hemingway, John L. "Leisure and Civility: Reflections on A Greek Ideal." *Leisure Studies*, vol. 10, 1988, pp. 179–91.

Holba, Annette. *Philosophical Leisure: Recuperative Practice for Human Communication*. Marquette University Press, 2007.

Holt, Jason. "Existential Ethics: Where the Paths of Glory Lead." *The Philosophy of Stanley Kubrick*, edited by Jerrold J. Abrams, University Press of Kentucky, 2007, pp. 49–56.

——. "Horses as Players in Equine Sports." *Sport, Ethics and Philosophy*, vol. 17, no. 4, 2023, pp. 456–64. https://doi.org/10.1080/17511321.2023.2189291

——. *Kinetic Beauty: The Philosophical Aesthetics of Sport*. Routledge, 2020.

——. "The Philosopher's Stallone: Significance of the *Rocky IV* Training Montage." *Cinematic Codes Review*, vol. 2, no. 1, 2017, pp. 61–67.

——. "Physical Philosophy: Martial Arts as Embodied Wisdom." *Philosophies*, vol. 8, no. 1, 2023, pp. 1–7. https://doi.org/10.3390/philosophies8010014

——. "Sport as Art, Dance as Sport." *Acta Universitatis Carolinae Kinanthropologica*, vol. 53, no. 2, 2017, pp. 138–45. https://doi.org/10.14712/23366052.2017.11

——. "Virtual Domains for Sports and Games." *Sport, Ethics and Philosophy*, vol. 10, no. 1, 2016, pp. 5–13. https://doi.org/10.1080/17511321.2016.1163729

——. "'Wayne's World' and the Philosophy of Play." *"Saturday Night Live" and Philosophy: Deep Thoughts Through the Decades*, edited by Jason Southworth and Ruth Tallman, Wiley-Blackwell, 2020, pp. 131–40.

Holt, Jason, and Robert Pitter. "The Prostitution Trap of Elite Sport in *He Got Game*." *The Philosophy of Spike Lee*, edited by Mark T. Conard, University Press of Kentucky, 2011, pp. 15–25.

Huizinga, Johan. *Homo Ludens: A Study of the Play-Element in Culture*. Beacon, 1955.

Krein, Kevin, and Jesús Ilundáin. "*Mushin* and Flow: An East-West Comparative Analysis." *Philosophy and the Martial Arts: Engagement*, edited by Graham Priest and Damon Young, Routledge, pp. 139–64.

Lao Tzu. *Tao Te Ching*. Translated by Jonathan Star, Tarcher, 2008.

Linder, Staffan Burenstam. *The Harried Leisure Class*. Columbia University Press, 1970.

Loy, Jr., John W. "The Nature of Sport: A Definitional Effort." *Philosophy of Sport: Core Readings*, edited by Jason Holt, 2nd ed., Broadview Press, 2022, pp. 39–57.

Meier, Klaus V. "Triad Trickery: Playing with Sports and Games." *Journal of the Philosophy of Sport*, vol. 15, 1988, pp. 11–30.

Meynell, Letitia, and Clarisse Paron. *Applied Ethics Primer*. Broadview Press, 2023.

Mill, John Stuart. *On Liberty*. Walter Scott Publishing, 2019.

——. *Utilitarianism*. The Floating Press, 2009.

Mumford, Stephen. "Russell's Defence of Idleness." *Russell: The Journal of Bertrand Russell Studies*, vol. 28, no. 1, 2008, pp. 5–19.

Naidoo, Maliga. "Leisure in Africa." *Leisure Matters: The State and Future of Leisure Studies*, edited by Gordon J. Walker, David Scott, and Monika Stodolska, Venture, 2016, pp. 93–100.

Nash, Jay B. *Philosophy of Recreation and Leisure*. W.C. Brown, 1960.

Nietzsche, Friedrich. *The Gay Science*. Translated by Walter Kaufmann, Vintage, 1974.

——. *On the Genealogy of Morals*. Translated by Douglas Smith, Oxford University Press, 1996.

O'Connor, Brian. *Idleness: A Philosophical Essay*. Princeton University Press, 2018.

Osborne, Richard, and Borin van Loon. *Introducing Eastern Philosophy*. Totem Books, 2006.

Parker, Stanley. *The Future of Work and Leisure*. Routledge, 1971.

Pieper, Josef. *Leisure the Basis of Culture*. Ignatius Press, 2009.

Plato. *The Laws*. Translated by Trevor J. Saunders, Penguin, 2004.

Ramsay, Hayden. *Reclaiming Leisure: Art, Sport and Philosophy*. Palgrave, 2005.

Rice, Brian. "Beyond Competition: An Indigenous Perspective on Organized Sport." *Decolonizing Sport*, edited by Janice Forsyth, Christine O'Bonsawin, Russell Field, and Murray G. Phillips, Fernwood Publishing, 2023, pp. 22–34.

Russell, Bertrand. *"In Praise of Idleness" and Other Essays*. Routledge, 2004.

Russell, J.S. "Idleness as Play and Leisure: A Reflection on *Idleness: A Philosophical Essay* by Brian O'Connor." *American Journal of Play*, vol. 14, no. 3, 2022, pp. 304–26.

——. "Idleness Would Be Preferred over Game Playing as an Ideal in Suits' Utopia." *Journal of the Philosophy of Sport*, vol. 49, no. 3, 2022, pp. 398–413. https://doi.org/10.1080/00948705.2022.2153692

Sartre, Jean-Paul. *Being and Nothingness: An Essay on Phenomenological Ontology*. Translated by Hazel E. Barnes, Routledge, 2005.

——. *Existentialism Is a Humanism*. Translated by Carol Macomber, Yale University Press, 2007.

Schneider, Angela J., and Robert B. Butcher. "Pre-lusory Goals for Games: A Gambit Declined." *Journal of the Philosophy of Sport*, vol. 24, 1997, pp. 38–46.

Seneca. "On Leisure." Translated by Timothy Chandler, *Colloquy: Text, Theory, Critique*, vol. 23, 2012, pp. 214–22.

Suits, Bernard. "The Elements of Sport." *The Philosophy of Sport: A Collection of Critical Essays*, edited by Robert G. Osterhoudt and Charles C. Thomas, 1973, pp. 48–64.

——. *The Grasshopper: Games, Life and Utopia*. 2nd ed., Broadview Press, 2005.

——. "Tricky Triad: Games, Play and Sport." *Journal of the Philosophy of Sport*, vol. 15, 1988, pp. 1–9.

——. "Words on Play." *Journal of the Philosophy of Sport*, vol. 4, no. 1, 1977, pp. 117–31.

Suzuki, D.T. *Zen Buddhism: Selected Writings of D.T. Suzuki*, edited by William Barrett, Doubleday, 1996.

Telfer, Elizabeth. "Leisure." *Royal Institute of Philosophy Supplements*, vol. 22, 1987, pp. 151–64.

Trainer, Chad. "In *Further* Praise of Idleness." *Russell Revisited: Critical Reflections on the Thought of Bertrand Russell*, edited by Alan Schwerin, Cambridge Scholars, 2008, pp. 115–25.

Veblen, Thorstein. *The Theory of the Leisure Class*. Oxford University Press, 2007.

Wang, Jianyu, and L. Allison Stringer. "The Impact of Taoism on Chinese Leisure." *World Leisure Journal*, vol. 42, no. 3, 2000, pp. 33–41. https://doi.org/10.1080/04419057.2000.9674194

Wetmore, Jr., Kevin J. "The Tao of 'Star Wars,' Or, Cultural Appropriation in a Galaxy Far, Far Away." *Studies in Popular Culture*, vol. 23, no. 1, 2000, pp. 91–106.

Wilde, Oscar. *The Picture of Dorian Gray*. Arcturus, 2009.

Wittgenstein, Ludwig. *Philosophical Investigations*. Blackwell, 1953.

Yeh, Chih-Kuei, and Garry Chick. "*Hsiao Yao*: A Chinese Analog of the Classical Western Idea of Leisure." *Leisure Sciences*, 2021, pp. 1–13. https://doi.org/10.1080/01490400.2021.1987360

Index

About the Publisher

The word "broadview" expresses a good deal of the philosophy behind our company. Our focus is very much on the humanities and social sciences—especially literature, writing, and philosophy—but within these fields we are open to a broad range of academic approaches and political viewpoints. We strive in particular to produce high-quality, pedagogically useful books for higher education classrooms—anthologies, editions, sourcebooks, surveys of particular academic fields and sub-fields, and also course texts for subjects such as composition, business communication, and critical thinking. We welcome the perspectives of authors from marginalized and underrepresented groups, and we have a strong commitment to the environment. We publish English-language works and translations from many parts of the world, and our books are available world-wide; we also publish a select list of titles with a specifically Canadian emphasis.

broadview press

This book is made of paper from well-managed FSC® - certified forests, recycled materials, and other controlled sources.